REIGNING WITH CHRIST
Ours is the Kingdom

by Justin V. Edmondson

DORRANCE
PUBLISHING CO
EST. 1920
PITTSBURGH, PENNSYLVANIA 15238

Dorrance Publishing Co
585 Alpha Drive
Suite 103
Pittsburgh, PA 15238
Visit our website at *www.dorrancebookstore.com*

ISBN: 978-1-6393-7117-4
eISBN: 978-1-6393-7929-3

DEDICATION

To my mother, Sylvia Edmondson, who has gone to be with the Lord but has taught me all I needed to know for Godly living. This book and all that I am was birthed from her teachings.

ACKNOWLEDGMENTS

I want to first acknowledge the Holy Spirit for his inspiration in me writing this book. He has imparted much revelation and direction, and I believe this is just the beginning. I would also like to thank my wife, children, and extended family for their support in me writing this book and my ministry. Special thanks to my niece, Fradian Murray, for assisting with editing and supporting my vision.

CONTENTS

INTRODUCTION

To reign with Christ on earth is to actively operate in his kingdom. For instance, healing the sick, raising the dead, interceding for souls, feeding the poor, following the leading of the Holy Spirit and financing the kingdom. These are all parts of the operations of the kingdom of God on earth, and all believers are responsible for carrying out these until Christ returns for his church. "And the Lord said, Who, then is that faithful and wise steward, whom his lord shall make ruler over his household, to give them their portion of meat in due season? Blessed is that servant, whom his lord when he cometh shall find so doing," according to Luke 12:42-43 (KJV).

However, despite the word of God many Christians believe that only when they die and get to heaven, they will reign with Christ. In my opinion, such belief produces believers who are only fit for heaven, unable to function in Christ's authority in the earth realm. As a result, I find that believers are easily overpowered by darkness, because they do not know their rights in Christ Jesus. Jesus declared in Luke 10:19(KJV), "Behold, I give unto you power to tread on serpents and scorpions, and over all the power of the enemy: and nothing shall by any means hurt you."

This scripture underscores that believers have spiritual authority over the kingdom of darkness which includes Satan and his demons. Here and now our responsibility as believers is to take action against the enemy by "casting down imaginations, and every high thing that exalteth itself against the knowledge of God and bringing into captivity every thought to the obedience of Christ" (see 2 Corinthians 10:5 KJV).

Are you using this authority? If you are not using it, is it because you think you do not have it or are you conscious of it but lack knowledge of how to use it? A sister in the church asked me to pray for her daughter who was being oppressed by demons. When I went in prayer the Holy Spirit told me that the sister had already prayed and that her payer was already answered. I instantly felt in my spirit the freedom of an answered prayer. When we go to God in prayer, we must believe that he hears us or else the devil will make us believe that God does not hear us; so, we will go around asking everybody to pray for us, when we have the authority in Christ to do so for ourselves. Matthew 16:19 (KJV) says, "And I will give unto thee the keys of the kingdom of heaven: and whatsoever thou shalt bind on earth shall be bound in heaven: and whatsoever thou shalt loose on earth shall be loosed in heaven."

While we want to reign on earth and should reign on earth, we should remember that this is not our final home. We were told to die, live, and endure with Christ to reign with him in eternity in 2 Timothy 2:11(KJV).

As you read this book ask the Lord to open your heart and your understanding to receive what he is saying to the church. I hope you will get a greater understanding of what it means to live in Christ, what is expected of us and the resources we have at our disposal to ensure that we live full Christian lives.

CHAPTER ONE
Reigning with Christ While on Earth

The idea of reigning with Christ is not a fantasy, but the reality and foundation of our Christian faith and our ultimate anticipation. As Christians we believe that we are reigning with Christ now in the spirit while awaiting his physical return as he promised. However, when most people think of reigning with Christ, the first thing that comes to mind is death, but this is not the case. The moment we accept Jesus as our Lord and savior we become a part of his body which gives us access and the privilege of becoming sons and daughters of God. Upon receiving His salvation, the Christian experience becomes a lifestyle modeled by the life of Christ. Throughout several scriptures we see God telling his people that as a blessing they will reign over others but if they disobeyed him, others would reign over them. This suggests that the will of God is for his people who trust and obey him to reign in the earth. After all, he told Adam that he had dominion over all living things in the earth. It is God's desire that we not only reign in heaven, but on earth. It is his delight that we subdue the earth, being lenders and not borrowers, prosperous and not beggars, full of the spirit and not of the flesh, hopeful and not hopeless, faithful, and not faithless. This was his desire before the creation of the world and this has not changed, our God remains the same yesterday, today and forever.

What It Means to Reign
According to the Merriam-Webster Dictionary, to reign means to possess or exercise sovereign power or authority; to rule; to exercise government, as a king or emperor; or to hold the supreme power over the universe. This is

Christ's risen position in heaven, on earth and under the earth. A position he only attained after his death. After his resurrection Christ declared, all power is given to me in heaven and on earth. He then commissioned his disciples to go and preach the gospel to all nations, and to perform baptisms in the name of the Father, Son, and Holy Spirit (see Matthew 28:18-20 KJV). Only a person with authority could give such command. With this commission came the assurance of his presence, I am with you always (Matthew 28:20 KJV).

In history books we read of great kings who rose and conquered nations and kingdoms, establishing thriving economies to generate wealth beyond imagination. Such kings included Nebuchadnezzar, king of Babylon who reigned from 605-562 B.C. As the longest reigning, and most powerful monarch, there was also Mongol leader Genghis Khan, who reigned from 1162-1227 and established the largest land empire in history in Asia and China. But even with all of this great wealth, power and accomplishments, I have never read nor seen any live long enough to sustain their kingdom pass a certain time because of their sinful and limited nature. However, there is a king who died to put off the robe of death for all mankind, he rose from the dead so we might live. "For God so loved the world, that he gave his only begotten Son, that whosoever believeth on him should not perish, but have eternal life" (see John 3:16 KJV). Today, He is above all and greater than all through His death. God has given him a name that is above every name that at the name of Jesus all things are under subjection (see Philippians 2:9 and Ephesians 1:22 KJV). Nonetheless, all are called to live and reign with him here and now and through eternity. Our reign in Christ is promised to be sustained. Our mortality does not limit our reign but sets us up for our ultimate authority, to reign in heavenly places. God has already given us the permission to represent him on earth, but how are we expected to reign? We are expected to die with him, live with him and endure so that we can reign in him (see 2 Timothy 2:11 KJV).

Realizing Our Need for God

Before we can begin reigning on earth, we must acknowledge that we need a savior—we need God. To conclude that we need God in our lives can be difficult because of our human nature. Often, we feel we are able to figure life out on our own. But how much of life do we really know? For us to claim that we can make it without God, we must be able to take ourselves from the dry and hard places where many of us are currently stuck. Some Christians loosely and fluidly depend on God because they are not privy to how God will work things out for them. One day they believe he is in control, the next day they doubt his power. It is not for us to know the "HOW," but it is for us to trust God when we cannot see how. Our need for God is greater than we can imagine, yet so many lack the desire to seek him. Jeremiah 29:13(KJV) says, "And ye shall seek me, and find me, when ye shall search for me with all your heart."

To get God's attention you must be real and transparent before him. It is okay to tell God that we worry about how he is going to do 'it' (whatever your 'it' is) and that the unknown is scary. He wants us to be bare before him. We are also expected to have a repentant heart, knowing that our need for him is greater than anything we can imagine. Many believers are struggling in their faith because they are yet to realize that they are a part of a kingdom that does not operate the way the world's system does. As a result, they live a Christian life operated through the natural, rather than a spiritual one. 1 Corinthians 2:14(KJV) says, "But the natural man received not the things of the Spirit of God: for they are foolishness unto him: neither can he know them, because they are spiritually discerned." God does not operate in the natural flesh-driven happenings, so he gave us the Holy Spirit to allow us constant fellowship with him. You will not find God in the things of this world, only in the spirit. To reign with him you must live in the spirit. This is where God sustains and keeps us from the power of darkness. To sustain means to maintain and keep alive. Spiritually speaking, all living things are on a life support system, including angels. We all rely on God to sustain and keep us whether we know it or not. When people are spiritually dead it is impossible for them to know this truth, they are likened to those who are on life support in the hospital but have no idea that it is a machine that is keeping them alive. They lack consciousness of the fact that the support system can be taken away at any time. But those who understand and know that God is the ultimate life support system look to God for help, because he is the source of life.

To reign with Christ your life must be sustained by his life, from his perspectives through faith and fellowship with him. Christ tells us that without him we can do nothing. John 15:2(KJV) says, "Every branch in me that beareth not fruit he taketh away: and every branch that beareth fruit, he purgeth it, that it may bring forth more fruit." Therefore, we need him every step of the way to make it in this life. Just as the grass and flower needs the sun and rain to grow, so we need him to survive. Acts 17:28(KJV) reads, "For in him we live, and move, and have our being; as certain also of your own poets have said, for we are also his offspring."

Hence, we need the breath of God to breathe on us. The breath of God, the Holy Spirit, is who keeps us in the will of God. When Jesus rose from the dead, he promised his disciples that they would receive the Holy Spirit (see John 20:22 KJV). He was making a new people who could accomplish and facilitate the will of God in the earth. To breathe on or into someone is to give them life, when God breathes on us, he transforms our lives, making us capable of operating effectively in his kingdom.

Living from God's Perspective

To reign with Christ, we must willingly observe his perspectives, because the kingdom and the power belongs to him, and only he knows best. People generally like to follow their own initiative on what they think is suitable, and oftentimes the effects are devastating. For example, a supervisor told the story of how one of his employees got fired on the spot because he broke a protocol. He was told to work on the eastside but instead, he worked on the westside. When the city inspector came to verify the work done, he found that he was out of compliance. Consequently, the company received a huge fine, because someone decided to do what he wanted rather than following the assignment given.

To reign with Christ, we must realize our need to live from God's perspective. Perspective is having the capacity to view things in their true relations or relative importance. What is God's perspective? God's perspective is revealed in his purpose for creating all living things which complement each other but only exist through him. People often abuse things and each other because they are either unappreciative or unaware of the value or the purpose of the thing or each other. The church was despised and rejected by both the Jews and Gentiles, and today it is the bedrock of most societies. Man sees the church and Christendom as a threat to liberalism, but God sees it as the only hope for mankind.

While we all have our own perspectives on life, it is limited and often misleading. The truth is, we do not know everything and are therefore prone to making mistakes which often causes us much regret. Some of us like to think that our way of doing things is the best approach. We want to be in control. But sadly, for us, the human's perspective is limited but God's perspective is unlimited. God told Abraham that his children would be enslaved by a strange nation even before Abraham's lineage came into existence. God also promised to deliver them out of said slavery even before they were enslaved, which followed after the death of Joseph in Egypt. Some might ask why God allowed them to be enslaved in the first place, when he could have prevented it. Yes, he could have prevented it, he had the power to, but God allowed it. His words will always come to pass. "For my thoughts are not your thoughts, neither are your ways my ways, saith the Lord. For as the heavens are higher than the earth, so are my ways higher than your ways, and my thoughts than your thoughts," according to Isaiah 55:8-9 (KJV).

God sometimes allows us to go through hard times when we refuse to submit our will to his, until we acknowledge our need for him. It is not uncommon that people neglect God when things are going well for them but revert to pursuing him when their backs are against the wall. However, God is not partial in allowing us to go through the refiner's fire. Scriptures, history, and modern-day testimonies have shown that it is only through pain and suffering that mankind truly turns to God. Scriptures show that whenever Israel sinned against God their enemies prevailed over them, but when they cried out to the Lord, he rose to deliver and help them (see Judges 2:11-17 (KJV).

When I started having children, I realized how much we hurt God when we decide not to follow his will for our lives. No matter how hard we try to lead and guide our families, some will end up doing their own thing which often leads them on a path of sorrow. One of my sons decided not to go to college after high school because he wanted to work. Irrespective of how I tried to dissuade him and tried to make him see that he was making a bad decision, he would not listen. He thought that his perspective on life was right, and that he knew what was best for himself. After working for a while, he had the crude awakening that minimum wage could not pay the bills, he needed more than a high school diploma to make his way comfortably in life. Him coming to the realization that he was wrong was good, but he could have been spared the harsh realities had he listened. God's plan for us is greater than our minds can fathom and often we miss it because we want to do it on our own.

When we follow God, we can never go wrong, no matter how difficult life gets his presence makes our problems seem like nothing. God knows the way we ought to take and his will for us is always good. However, there are many things that will try to prevent you from becoming who God says you are, it is the war of the flesh and the spirit. It is integral that your mind be made up, come what may, to face the challenges that are being put in place to sabotage your life. The spirit of sabotage is real; therefore, you must be a real fighter. If God said it, no power on earth or hell can stop it, if God wants it for us, we should also want it. Your desperation for the will of God will determine how soon you will be made aware of it. Jeremiah 29:11-13(KJV)says, "For I know the thoughts that I think toward you, saith the Lord, thoughts of peace, and not of evil, to give you an expected end. Then shall ye call upon me, and ye shall go and pray unto me, and I will hearken unto you. And ye shall seek me, and find me, when ye shall search for me with all your heart."

The devil will try to use a man or woman or things to derail you from fulfilling God's purpose, which is God's greatest perspective for our lives. God wants us to live purposeful lives, knowing that we are not alone and that we will overcome (see 1 Peter 4:12-19).

Some of you have great dreams and aspirations including going to the moon, we see so many wealthy people doing this now. But some of your own family members have sabotaged your process and your walk-in purpose, and you feel like giving up. But God said to tell you, do not give up, use the interruption as the bridge to get over. Get into fasting and prayer, spend some time in God's presence, the giver of the calling and purpose. "Down on my knees when sorrows rise, I talk to Jesus down on my knees," according to the popular church hymn. In earlier times women would deliver babies while kneeling, this position encouraged movement of the baby. What is inside of you will take a kneeling position to get it out. Joseph was sold into slavery by his brothers because of his dream. However, God was with him in his darkest hour and made his life prosperous, so much so that Potiphar saw that God was with Joseph and that all he did prospered. So, he gave him control over all he had; not because of Joseph's ability but the fact that God was with him. This is what amazes me, when God is with you it brings promotion and prosperity that even those who are against you will recognize that you are blessed. Potiphar realized that he needed Joseph to make his life better, so he promoted him by making him the head of his house. He was a smart businessman who was willing to demote himself to accumulate wealth and power because he saw that God was with Joseph (see Genesis 39:6 KJV). His wife realized that the new wealth was coming from Joseph, so her mind shifted from Potiphar to Joseph because she was in it for what she could get. When she told Joseph to lay with her (Genesis 39:7 KJV), she thought she would be able to manipulate him, if he had succumbed, he would have killed the source of power. Joseph instead sternly asked, "How then could I do such a wicked thing and sin against God?" (Genesis 39:9 NIV). He saw the act as sinning against God, not as pleasure. Whenever you see sin as pleasure you are sure to fail. When a man or a woman looks at a person and sees beauty, nothing is wrong with that, but the moment you see pleasure your soul is in trouble.

Some people are willing to do anything for a promotion, they will relinquish their dignity for more recognition. They will walk on others, lie on others, just to be seen or for a bigger paycheck. Joseph got a promotion, but he lost it. God did not give that promotion to Joseph, Potiphar did. When God gives you something no one can take it from you, not even the devil. When we run ahead and accept what God did not give us, it only sets us back. Joseph had to go back on the potter's wheel, on his knees again, because God was not finished with him. When we accept things that are not the will of God, he will have to burn them out of us. A pastor once told me when I was a traveling evangelist to come and join his church and he would open doors for me. He spoke as if he were God, I never answered him, and he never called me back to preach. When men promote you, they are sooner to demote you. When you wait on God, he will elevate you and no man can stop or relinquish your promotion.

God will allow things to happen that will take you to the top, just when you think it is over God will blow your mind and make you shiver down your spine in wonder. Joseph was in prison for rape, an act he did not commit. But that did not stop Potiphar from throwing Joseph into jail because his wife had evidence in her hands. Some people have chosen not to forgive you for things you have done ages ago. In fact, some have no proof that you did the thing that they are mad at you about, but you have received the blame. Pharaoh's butler and baker got in trouble with him, and he put them in prison where Joseph was. They both had a dream and was troubled, Joseph saw the sorrow on their faces, so he asked Pharaoh's officials who were in custody with him, "Why do you look so sad today?" "We both had dreams," they answered, "but there is no one to interpret them." Then Joseph said to them, "Do not interpretations belong to God? Tell me your dreams" (see Genesis 40:7-8 NIV). He interpreted their dreams, and they came out of prison as he told them. To them he was just a prisoner, but to God he was a precious jewel. Over two years passed after the butler was released before he remembered Joseph and it was not until the King had a dream which needed interpreting. God has a set time to loose you from whichever prison you are in, just follow his perspectives, and you will come out as a wonder in the hands of God. The only caveat is that we live from God's perspective, see through his eyes, see his will in where he has us, and constantly pursue him to be aware of what he wants.

Christ Is Our Model

We ought to model the life of Christ to die with him, live with him, endure and ultimately reign in him—He is our standard. Jesus knew that this world would be unaccommodating of the new kind of people he intended to make. The new creatures we were to be transformed into, would be challenged daily by the darkness of this world. We are likened to harmless and vulnerable sheep. We are in constant need of Christ's affection and guidance to survive among the modern temptations and established religions of this day, such as the Jewish religion, and that of the pagans. The Jewish religion was introduced to set apart God's people from the rest of the world, in designating worship exclusively to God. The pagans were known to have several gods, but the Jewish religion had only one God and this made it powerful. After the death of Moses, and Joshua (Moses' successor) the Jews slipped into idolatrous worship by worshiping pagan gods, as such God brought their dynasty of priests, prophets, and kings to an end and replaced it with one man, Jesus Christ. He is the ultimate priest, prophet, and king.

As the high priest he offers true sacrifices unto God without spot or blemish. The kind of sacrifice Israel could never have offered to God. What is a sacrifice? This is the act of giving up something precious though worth keeping, in order to scale back or to be able to do something else or to help someone. The Bible shares many examples of sacrifices which were offered to God, from Abel offering a sheep, to the rebuilding of the temple by Herod the Great in Jerusalem in 70 C.E. But all these sacrifices brought temporary redemption, leaving the offeror to return to offer again. But Jesus offered himself as a living sacrifice, in total surrender to the will of God, to satisfy the wrath of God that was against humanity. Hebrews 4:14-16(KJV) reads, "Seeing then that we have a great high priest, that is passed into the heavens, Jesus the Son of God, let us hold fast our profession. For we have not a high priest which cannot be touched with the feeling of our infirmities; but was in all points tempted like as we are, yet without sin. Let us therefore come boldly unto the throne of grace, that we may obtain mercy, and find grace to help in time of need." We ought to recognize that we have a compassionate priest of whom we can find atonement. As believers we are expected to be unrestrained by sin but boldly holding to our faith and holiness while being confident of grace when we mess up. Without acceptance of this position of Christ and our access to this authority, we will never reign in Christ.

As a prophet he precisely declares the will of God to his people of things past, present and things to come, since he was commissioned by God to proclaim his will for mankind. Jesus did just that, and the Sanhedrin condemned him to death because they were opposed to the ways of God. A prophet is inspired and sent by God to proclaim his will. Isaiah 61:1-3(KJV) says, "The Spirit of the Lord GOD is upon me; because the LORD hath anointed me to preach good tidings unto the meek; he hath sent me to bind up the brokenhearted, to proclaim liberty to the captives, and the opening of the prison to them that are bound. To proclaim the acceptable year of the LORD, and the day of vengeance of our God; to comfort all that mourn; To appoint unto them that mourn in Zion, to give unto them beauty for ashes, the oil of joy for mourning, the garment of praise for the spirit of heaviness; that they might be called trees of righteousness, the planting of the LORD, that he might be glorified."

Through Christ we have access to the will of God concerning us, we are not kept in the dark on the plans he has for us. We know that he is coming back for us, we know that we will be judged according to the lives we lead. By this revelation and our access to the prophecies of God, we are inspired daily to live lives worthy of heaven. Jesus is willing to reveal all things to us so that we can prosper in this life. We too must be willing to proclaim the gospel to the world. Some of us think that means traveling to another country on mission trips, but how often do we witness to our unsaved family members? Are we a source of comfort to our mourning neighbors?

As king he is the ruler of the universe whose kingdom cannot be taken away or replaced. He is King of kings and Lord of lords. As king he conquered death, and hell. After the fall of Adam and Eve death and hell became man's inheritance, but in love and mercy Christ took our place. 2 Corinthians 5:21 (KJV) says, "For he hath made him to be sin for us, who knew no sin; that we might be made the righteousness of God in him." In every earthly kingdom man die for their kings, but Christ the King of glory died for us. John 15:13(KJV) reads, "Greater love hath no man than this, that a man lay down his life for his friends." Now we are called upon to lay down our lives for him so that we too may conquer death and hell through him.

The Gift of the Holy Spirit

Christ's personhood in the form of flesh was limited by his death. He came on earth as the ultimate sacrifice personifying what it means to reign on earth, while being priest, prophet, and king. But he had to ascend to the Father to fulfill his role of intercessor. I know most of us would have wished to have been there while he was on earth, we wish we had access to him the way the disciples did. Some of us would have been like Mary, hugging his feet, neglecting the cares of life just to be in his presence. But our God made sure we could all carry his presence by sending the Holy Spirit. We can reign in Christ the way the disciples did and all who encountered him, daily through the infilling of the Holy Spirit.

Christ has granted us access to the Father through his blood and the Holy Spirit who is our comforter, to preserve and keep us while we are in this world. To reign with Christ, you must have the Holy Spirit; if you do not have him, you are not a child of God. The world is filled with wickedness and therefore the Holy Spirit came to guide and help us into all truth. To gain access to him you must first receive Christ. The moment that you accept Christ as your Lord and Savior the Holy Spirit comes and dwells in you. Hence, all believers have the Holy Spirit living in them as the Spirit of Truth. John 16:13 (KJV) reads,

"Howbeit when he, the Spirit of truth, is come, he will guide you into all truth: for he shall not speak of himself; but whatsoever he shall hear, that shall he speak: and he will shew you things to come."

The Holy Spirit is God. Therefore, when we approach him, we should do so with reverence, respect and worship. He is a person, with wisdom, understanding, counsel, fortitude, knowledge, piety, and the fear of the Lord. When Jesus purchased our redemption, he sealed us with the Holy Spirit, and gave us all the attributes of the Spirit. The manifestation of the Holy Spirit signals to the world that we belong to him and are his. As such, we are restored to the Father when we receive Christ as our Lord and Savior. Therefore, believers should walk in the attributes of the Holy Spirit because these set us apart from the world.

The Holy Spirit was given as our helper, to help us navigate life. Having the Holy Spirit benefits us in more ways than we can image. He helps us to make sound judgments, and he helps us to see God as our Father and others as our brothers and sisters regardless of the color of their skin. He helps us to choose good over evil in our daily lives and causes us to walk in obedience to the Father and aids us in our worship of God in spirit and in truth. Some claim to be wise and yet oppress the poor and take from the less fortunate, indicating that they do not have the wisdom of God to resist evil and choose good. Wisdom is having experience, knowledge, and good judgment in circumstances, providing a solution or an action. We are constantly faced with opportunities which require us to make wise decisions. Some people make decisions based on their feelings without looking at the positive and negative effects of their choices. Some of us are emotionally led, instead of Spirit led. But the Holy Spirit was given to us to guide us in all truth and not fluctuating emotions. Many claim to have wisdom, but true wisdom comes from knowing God. A true show of wisdom is your decision to serve God because you have recognized that there is a God. When we look at all his wonders surrounding us, and his goodness towards people, these demonstrations make us marvel at his greatness. Wisemen came from far countries, saying, "Where is he that is born King of the Jews? For we have seen his star in the east and are come to worship him" (see Matthew 2:2KJV). Wise people seek after God because they know the importance of having God in their lives.

Furthermore, the Holy Spirit teaches us how to live as Christians. We live in a world that is filled with confusion, immorality, and conflicting behaviors, which the culture portrays as right living. The gift of understanding enables our apprehension of truth and leads us in the right path. As such, the Apostle Paul prayed Ephesians 1:18(KJV):"The eyes of your understanding being enlightened; that ye may know what the hope of his calling is, and what the riches of the glory of his inheritance in the saints." To step out in faith, believers our spiritual understanding must be opened in order to differentiate the will of the Father from the ways of the world. It is only through the spirit of understanding that we reign with Christ and comprehend the mysteries of the gospel. The Holy Spirit's role is very important in the life of the believer, so much so that if a person does not have the Holy Spirit, he or she does not have God. People of all ages will tell you that we are all children of God but in the eyes of God only those who are born of the Spirit are children of God. The gift of the Holy Spirit enables our apprehension of this truth, that we are to be set apart.

The power of the Holy Spirit is the power of God and is not to be played with or despised. The Spirit, the third person of the Trinity has appeared throughout scripture as a person who performed great works by his power. His presence was first seen in the act of creation, for it was by his power the world came into being (see Genesis 1:1-2 NIV). The Holy Spirit also empowered men in the Old Testament to accomplish God's will; Moses was impowered by the Holy Spirit to bring the children out of bondage. Aaron's rod turned into a serpent and swallowed the power of Egypt (see Exodus 7:10-12). Although the Spirit did not permanently dwell with God's people in the Old Testament, He worked through them and gave them power to achieve things they would not have been able to accomplish on their own. David killed Goliath with a stone (see 1 Samuel 17:49), after Samuel anointed him as king of Israel, the Holy Spirit came upon him and remained with him (see 1 Samuel 16:13). ˙

Jesus promised us that the Spirit would be a permanent guide, teacher, seal of salvation, and comforter for the believers(see John 14:26). He also promised that the Holy Spirit's power would help His followers to spread the message of the gospel around the world: "But you will receive power when the Holy Spirit comes on you; and you will be my witnesses in Jerusalem, and in all Judea and Samaria, and to the ends of the earth," according to Acts 1:8 (NIV).

God has given us all we need to reign with him and through him, he is our model, our perfect example for Godly and fruitful living. It is high time that we walk boldly and securely in the guidance of the Holy Spirit.

We have looked at how God has set us up to reign in him while on earth, we will now look at what qualifies us to reign in him for eternity.

CHAPTER TWO

Dying with Christ

The fact that all was sentenced to death because of Adam's disobedience, created a need for life. Christ's death gives us life, by taking our place on the cross he became the clause to our death sentence. 2 Corinthians 5:21(NIV) says, "God made him who had no sin to be sin for us, so that in him we might become the righteousness of God." His death destroyed the power of sin and opened the gate of heaven that all may go in. Satan, the chief priests, the people of Jerusalem and the Roman procreator all thought it was over when they nailed him to the cross. He cried, "It is finished" (see John 19:30 KJV), and gave up the ghost to secure our redemption. Three days later, he rose from death. "O death, where is thy sting? O grave, where is thy victory? The sting of death is sin; and the strength of sin is the law. But thanks be to God, which giveth us the victory through our Lord Jesus Christ" (1 Corinthians 15:55-57KJV). Jesus won the victory over death and hell so that all who believe in him might live to the glory of God the Father. After his resurrection he ascended into heaven to sit at the right hand of God. He was seen by his disciples and over five hundred people as he ascended. Similar to his transfiguration on the mount, Jesus displayed to man that he was divine and that there was a greater glory beyond the earth. These public acts give us assurance that he reigns as God.

Jesus emptied himself by becoming man (see Philippians 2:7 KJV) without marring his Godly nature so that we may have untethered access to the throne. He became the ultimate high priest, offering open communion to all who would freely receive it. Through this grace of a new covenant, we can access heaven daily, hourly, minutely. This grace nullifies the dependency on our pastors and leaders but affords us the privilege to know God for ourselves. To reign with God on earth and ultimately in heaven we must accept this grace, we must understand the finished work of the cross and what it meant as the veil was torn in the temple (see Matthew 27:51) and exploit the bold access we now have to the throne and the Father. Reigning with Christ requires that we regularly enter the Holy of Holies which his redemptive blood affords us.

Putting God First

Christ is victorious, he overcame all odds which were against him. He has accomplished what Moses and the prophets could not have done by offering himself, wholly submitted to the Father's will. Rather than give an offering to God, as men traditionally did, he offered himself as that sacrifice. He knew the Father's will and was willing to pay the price. Many of us know what the Father needs of us, yet we prefer to please ourselves by putting our jobs, our families, our businesses, our time, and our money first. At the age of twelve Jesus was already purpose driven, his parents sought for him and found him among the lawyers and teachers of the law. Jesus said unto them, "How is it that ye sought me? Wist ye not that I must be about my Father's business?" (see Luke 2:49 KJV).

Putting God first means he has an open invitation in all your affairs. As Proverbs 3:6 (KJV) states, "In all thy ways acknowledge him, and he shall direct thy path." You can never go wrong when you put your trust in the all-knowing God. God has given us the privilege to approach him whenever we desire. Knowing that he is right there when you need him is more than anyone could ask. In return, all he asks of us is to be there for him in worship, fellowship, and communion. All these things God desires of us as his children. Christ knew the Father's heart and was willing to suffer humiliation to restore us to him, and we must do the same. "If we suffer, we shall also reign with him: if we deny him, he also will deny us," says 2 Timothy 2:12 (KJV).

Every day we are faced with the choice of whether to invest time and energy in God's kingdom or the kingdom of darkness. So many have wasted their time investing their resources in this world, which provides no security for their souls. When you put your trust in God you are divinely secure. We are heirs to the victory that Christ won on calvary. No matter what comes your way, life, or death, you have already won through Christ Jesus. Romans 8:37 (KJV) says, "Nay, in all these things we are more than conquerors through him that loved us."

Confession of Sins and True Repentance

As children of God, we must live in consistent, confession and repentance to God for our sins and shortcomings. This act of confession is a sort of killing of our flesh. It signifies to God that we recognize we need his saving grace. Consistent repentance of sins allows us to be in consistent fellowship with Christ since our sins separate us from him. James 4:8 (NIV) reads, "Come near to God and he will come near to you. Wash your hands, you sinners, and purify your hearts, you double-minded. "True repentance says to God that we acknowledge our sins, and we are turning from them.

Proverbs 28:13(KJV) says, "He that covereth his sins shall not prosper: but whoso confesseth and forsaketh them shall have mercy." Oftentimes we confess our sins but neglect to forsake them, we feel the guilt of them, but the associated pleasures often keep us chained. "If we claim to have fellowship with God and yet walk in the darkness, we lie and do not live out the truth. But if we walk in the light, as he is in the light, we have fellowship with one another, and the blood of Jesus, his Son, purifies us from all sin. If we claim to be without sin, we deceive ourselves and the truth is not in us. If we confess our sins, he is faithful and just and will forgive us our sins and purify us from all unrighteousness," according to 1 John 1: 6-9 (NIV).

Some people are going to church but are not experiencing the presence of God in their lives because they are not willing to confess, repent, and let go of the things of this world. God will separate himself from us if we continue in sin. 1 John 2:15 (KJV) reads, "Love not the world, neither the things that are in the world. If any man loves the world, the love of the Father is not in him." To embrace the presence of God you must be willing to separate yourself from things that do not represent God. The next verse of the same chapter (1 John 2:16 KJV) says, "For all that is in the world, the lust of the flesh, and the lust of the eyes, and the pride of life is not of the Father, but of the world." If we embrace the things of this world, we deny God. As such, some are in churches for many years, and still do not know who Jesus is.

When you live for God, your life will soar like the eagle, nothing will be impossible for the child of God who lives and reigns with Christ on earth. "For the Lord God is a sun and shield; the Lord will give grace and glory; no good thing will He withhold from them that walk uprightly," according to Psalm 84:11 (KJV). I often hear people ask why God is not blessing them, but our walk must be upright, meaning that God must be the center of our lives for us to fully receive his blessings. Eagles control their speed by the angling of their wings; our eyes must be fixed on God for us to maneuver the trials and difficulties we face in this life.

I make it a habit to confess sins in my life as soon as I recognize them before they take root. When unconfessed sins are in our lives, God does not hear our prayers. "If I regard iniquity in my heart, the Lord will not hear me," Psalm 66:18 (KJV). Our responsibility as children of God is to admit our faults before the Lord, and he will hear us when we call.

Sin hinders a believer's spiritual growth; it is therefore dangerous to walk around with unconfessed sin. It keeps your soul in bondage and facilitates a life of lies. I know of a young married man who spent most of his marriage cheating on his wife. Although she eventually caught up with him, he never confessed to her nor God. They eventually got a divorce. There is no help for people who do not see a fault in the way they are living. There can be no saving of those who are not willing to confess their sins to God and their need for him. While confession is important, true repentance is even more vital. We ought to turn from our sins, actively trying to live holy lives so that we can be worthy of our calling. How can we say we are heaven bound if we are living like the world, whether in secret or for everyone to see? How can God truly use us on earth to fulfill his glory if we are slaves to sin?

Becoming Dead to Sin

The one thing that keeps us from the presence of God is sin, it is the enemy of God. Sin prevents us from doing the will of God, as such we miss out on God's glory. Yes, we love God, that is why we got saved, frequent church, or tune in to religious services—but not to the point of death. We claim to love God, but we hardly do what he says, and this is sin. Sin wars against God and prevents us from fulfilling God's purpose, it leaves us bitter and revengeful, envious, prideful and prevents us from hearing God's voice. Therefore, to reign with him we must be dead to sin. Romans 8:7-8 (KJV) says, "Because the carnal mind is enmity against God: for it is not subject to the law of God, neither indeed can be. So, then they that are in the flesh cannot please God."

To be dead to sin means that a child of God ceases to live under the power of sin and according to the world's system, grasping fully that we are a new creation in Christ. We are then expected to live by the principles of God through his divine nature, as children of God. If we are not dead to sin, we are doomed to struggle against the sinful nature, since we were born in sin. Therefore, we must die for Christ to live in us and for us to live in him. Romans 8:13 (KJV) reads, "For if ye live after the flesh, ye shall die but if ye through the Spirit do mortify the deeds of the body, ye shall live." We cannot please God if we live by the flesh, God is a spirit, and he is holy and will not dwell in sin.

Therefore, to live a purpose driven life we must be dead to sin. We cannot operate in the Holy Spirit when sin controls us, Proverbs 14:34(KJV)says, "Righteousness exalted a nation: but sin is a reproach to any people." A purpose-driven life is a life that is set a part for his purpose. He can call on that life for any task, at any time without notice and without disappointment. Some of us require a week's notice before we can prepare a sermon, or before we can pray for someone. It is as though we must jump start our souls before we can go, possibly because they are corroded by sin. Believers must always be ready to share and demonstrate the gospel. The gospel is urgent, it is like the emergency room where sick people are constantly coming in with varied needs but requiring urgent care. Delay could cause someone their life. The doctor on the ward cannot tell a dying patient, "Let me go and check my textbooks and come back, then maybe I can diagnose your problem." He or she must always be ready to care for the sick. To be ready means to be prepared for any circumstance. Our embrace of sin limits the move of God in our lives and blocks our calling. People are literally dying in sin while we require and demand the perfect circumstance to share the gospel. While some of us may refrain from doing the work of God because we know that we are swimming in sin, there are others who do not mind. But since we are cultured to praise gifts, we end up supporting preachers and worship leaders who are also sinners, but there is no real move of God.

There is only one way to deal with sin, and it is through death. Believers can only truly live through the death of the flesh. God does not want us to give up stuff on his account, anything that you give up you can easily access again. A drug addict may give up drugs but sometimes when things get rough, he or she may go back to the old habit. God wants us to freely choose a life of purity and holiness.

God's prognosis for sin is death by crucifixion, it is the worst kind of death, but death is the punishment for sin. Because sin can cost us so much it is important that we expose and destroy it. Too many of us are guilty of trying to cover sin rather than exposing it. Through scriptures we see how God consistently wiped-out sin, it is clear that he hates it and we should too, both publicly and privately. When you hide sin, you protect and allow it to grow, the more it grows the harder it is to conceal it. As believers, we should follow God's principle for dealing with sin. The scripture says, "I am crucified with Christ: nevertheless, I live; yet not I, but Christ liveth in me: and the life which I now live in the flesh I live by the faith of the Son of God, who loved me, and gave himself for me," see Galatians 2:20 (KJV). We can only worship God in spirit and in truth only when sin is truly dead in us. If we harbor sin in our lives, it will prevent the Spirit of God to move in us. We must conclude that sin must die. Abraham was willing to offer Isaac his only son as an offering to God because he was dead to the sin of disobedience. When we are dead to sin, it makes it easier to please God without debating his will. People often murmur and complain when God speaks, an attitude promoted by the sin in their lives which strives only to resist the will of God. But when sin is dead you will automatically move in obedience whenever God speaks because your spirit, soul, mind, and body are subjected to God.

We Are No Longer Slaves to Sin

In heaven there is no sin, only the will of God. Sin is what is preventing us from seeing the manifestation of the glory of God. Whenever a believer completely surrenders his or her life to the Lord and forsakes sin God comes and dwells in this person's life. If sin is present in your life, you will only walk in a form of godliness with no power. A young Christian man shared his story of how he is struggling with an addiction to pornography. He shared that before he became a Christian, he would watch porn all the time, but this became more moderate when he got baptized. But the spirit would convict him every time he did it, yet he would ignore the prodding of the Holy Spirit. He continued to disregard the Holy Spirit, until he got out of tune with the faith and decided to stop going to church. He decided he would stay home and read his Bible since it was self-explanatory. The devil had blinded him, because he chose not to let go, and seek the Lord. Even if God sends someone to help him, he probably won't change, because he chose to be a slave to sin. If we allow sin in our lives, it will dominate us. We have a choice, sin is not our master, Jesus is!

A slave is someone who his bond to someone else's idea which they have adapted as their own. Slavery to sin persuades men to do evil and reject good. It controls the life of those who submit to it and convinces them that what they are doing is right.

There are many Christians who have stepped away from active service in the church because they refuse to let go of the sin in their lives. Some believe that if they stay away, they will not feel convicted or condemned. They believe they can do without the instructions of a teacher or preacher and they can hear from God by reading for themselves. James 5:16(KJV) says, "Confess your faults one to another, and pray one for another, that ye may be healed. The effectual fervent prayer of a righteous man availeth much." I prayed for the young man thinking he was willing to change and that he wanted to give it to the Lord, but that was not the case. He continued to feed the flesh rather than the spirit. "Be not deceived; God is not mocked: for whatsoever a man soweth, that shall he also reap. For he that soweth to his flesh shall of the flesh reap corruption; but he that soweth to the Spirit shall of the Spirit reap life everlasting," Galatians 6:7-8 (KJV).

God is light, and as such there is no darkness in him. If we live in him darkness will be exposed. Our responsibility as Christians is to confront sin and ask the Lord to remove it from our lives. It is his pleasure to make us holy, we are his children, and he loves us. No Father wants to see their children going down the wrong path or struggling in life especially after he has done all he can for them to live a bountiful life. God has given us all we need for righteous living, if we hold on to sin, we forfeit our authority as believers. Clinging to sin makes us of the world, preferring darkness than light. How can we then reign in Christ if we live as the world? How can we reign in Christ if we consistently yield to the flesh, making excuses for the sins thereof?

21

Children of God need to take their failures and weakness to the Lord in prayer and remain in prayer until things change. Too often we leave the altar with our problems instead of leaving them there, while the world's watching us carry our problems, yet we claim to know God. This makes our relationship with the Lord questionable. So often we take God for granted when things are going well, God is not needed until our backs are against the wall.

A man decided to pray only at nights, because he claimed that he could not find any other time, so he wakes in the morning get dressed and leaves for work. This was his lifestyle. One day his friend got into an altercation. He promised to give his friend a weapon to defend himself after the friend got into an argument at the work site. When we do not make time for God, we will make time for the devil. Someone had to step in and explain to him that we do not fight flesh and blood but spiritual wickedness. When we are not in relationship with God, sin becomes easy.

When we live from just the name Christian or a baptism, and not from a relationship with the person of Jesus Christ, the devil will cause us to sin against God. Many have discredited the name of Jesus and have brought reproach on the church because of their lack of commitment to God. Consequently, unbelievers have many negative remarks about the church of today.

The Bible tells us about a man who was cripple for thirty-eight years, lying by the pool waiting for the water to be troubled. He was in a religious community among people who claimed to have known God in a real way, but they were unable to help this man because the religious system that was designed to provide deliverance and to heal the sick and cleanse the lepers was crippled by sin. Even those who claimed to be whole were crippled by sin. Where do you go when the people of God cease to do the will of God? Many people are in our churches still waiting for God to move on their behalf and often they die without seeing their prayers answered or without any results. God is not at fault here, man is! The work is already completed in Christ Jesus but often those who are in leadership and dissemination of the word of God are deceitful and wicked. The command has been given, "Heal the sick, cleanse the lepers, raise the dead, cast out devils, freely ye have received, freely give," Matthew 10:8 (KJV). It is as clear as day that some people are preaching and teaching sermons without hearing anything from God. To be effective, one must be constantly receiving from God and many preachers only talk to God when they deem it necessary. There are some preachers who only resort to God when the church is not bringing in enough money to pay the bills or when their own child is sick, or a family member is dying. These are not the only time to pray, we must constantly live in his presence to draw from him.

To reign with Christ, you must be at peace with him. Sin separates us from our creator and robs us of intimacy with God. The man at the pool was not healed until he had an encounter with Christ. Jesus asked the impotent man at the pool of Bethesda, "...Wilt thou be made whole?" The impotent man answered him, "Sir, I have no man, when the water is troubled, to put me into the pool," see John 5:6-7 (KJV). Instead of looking to God for help he was looking to man. At times many are not healed because they are looking to man instead of God. Yes, God can use man to bring healing to your life and he often does so, but they are merely tools for his purpose—he is the giver of healing.

It is common to hear about seriously ill persons not giving up the will to live because they want another chance at life. A woman living in California with a family history of cancer went to see her doctor for a breast examination and found out she was without cancer. Out of fear she requested that the doctor cut off both breasts to prevent any cancerous growth because she saw what it did to her family. Usually when one has a physical disease, he or she becomes anxious to be made whole. But the truth is that there is a greater malignancy that is eating away at the souls of men and not everyone wishes to rid themselves of this loathsome disease called sin. Therefore, let us make spiritual application of this question asked by Jesus, "Wilt thou be made whole?"

Being Obedient and Committed to God

To walk with God you must be faithful, obedient, and willing, offering yourself to him without reservations. Once there is a split in leadership and room for a deputy, Satan will use it against you. This is one reason why Christians should live a committed life unto God. "Ye shall walk in all the ways which the Lord your God hath commanded you, that ye may live, and that it may be well with you, and that ye may prolong your days in the land which ye shall possess," according to Deuteronomy 5:33 (KJV). This verse highlights the way believers should live and in turn how he will bless and prosper those who remain faithful. This does not suggest a perfect life, but it will be better than if you do not walk in his ways. God will walk with us if we are obedient to His laws and statutes, but if we are not—God declares, "Then will I also walk contrary unto you and will punish you yet seven times for your sins," see Leviticus 26:24(KJV). Living a committed life can certainly be paired to walking in obedience in the ways of God.

When you commit your whole life, it becomes solely about God. With this mindset there is no place for the devil, your love for God completely stamps him out. Christianity is about being made one with God—this oneness should be the goal of every believer. Before the fall of mankind, God had a close, intimate relationship with Adam and Eve. They were in accordance with God's will until the day they chose for themselves the knowledge of what is good and what is evil. God withdrew himself from the presence of Adam and Eve because their sins had separated them from him (see Isaiah 59:2). There are somethings we indulge in and regard as "nothing," the little things we often label as "living," but God actually calls these sins. There are some believers who could never share their playlists since they are plagued with explicit lyrics, the movies they watch promote violence, murder, sexual pleasures, lust, and profanity. We must understand that words and images are seeds, and we should guard our ears and eyes. Christians should not indulge in the things of the world; this is not our kingdom. Our support of the world's culture will only hinder our spiritual growth and development and separate us from God since he said, "Be holy, because I am holy,"1 Peter 1:16 (NIV).

To reign with Christ man's will must be merged in God's. Your life must become his and his life must become yours. Philippians 2: 5-8 (KJV) reads, "Let this mind be in you, which was also in Christ Jesus: Who, being in the form of God, thought it not robbery to be equal with God: But made himself of no reputation, and took upon him the form of a servant, and was made in the likeness of men: And being found in fashion as a man, he humbled himself, and became obedient unto death, even the death of the cross." This process is painful and timely, because of our sinful nature it cannot be done overnight. For God to make us whole again and unto himself, he must fix us piece by piece. Each person who comes to Christ must go through this process of being made whole. Some people remain stuck because they stop the process instead of seeing it through. The process of becoming whole and one with God often includes us forgiving others. It requires that we are committed to the sifting and the transformative work of the Holy Spirit. One of the most popular scriptures, Matthew 6:12(KJV), says, "And forgive us our debts, as we forgive our debtors." This suggests that our forgiveness by God is tied to us forgiving others. Sometimes the hardest thing to do is to forgive, especially when we think the hurt was great. God will ask us to forgive even the person who hurt us the most, yet some of us will hold on to the painful memories and bitterness of unforgiveness despite hearing the Lord's voice to forgive. Us acknowledging what scripture says and applying them to our lives, are symbols of our commitment to God and our obedience to him. Disobedience to God will stop the process of us being one with him, God will not move forward until we obey him. This is just one reason why some people are not growing spiritually; they hinder the process that will make them free. Yet we walk around as if all is well, with the biggest praise and the loudest shout yet we are still in bondage with all kinds of problems, sicknesses, stress, and pain.

Our commitment, submission, and faithfulness to the will of God and his process of making us one with him is a step to reigning with him.

Never Look Back on What You Have Left

Indulging in a distraction is the process of forsaking what is purposeful and placing one's attention on other things; thereby blocking the reception of what is important. When you come to Jesus Christ never attempt to go back to your world of sin. "For it is impossible for those who were once enlightened, and have tasted of the heavenly gift, and were made partakers of the Holy Ghost. And have tasted the good word of God, and the powers of the world to come. If they shall fall away, to renew them again unto repentance; seeing they crucify to themselves the Son of God afresh and put him to an open shame" (see Hebrews 6:4-6 (KJV)).

Never look back means to show no sign of returning to past circumstances or allowing your past to define who you are. Countless people are looking back today because they have not decided to finish what they started. Looking back becomes the easy way out, instead of tailoring their future, they allow society to shape them. "And Jesus said unto him, no man, having put his hand to the plough, and looking back, is fit for the kingdom of God," see Luke 9:62 (KJV).

The thing that makes a believer fit for the kingdom is their ability to keep moving forward with the understanding that they may fracture a limb yet have no time to stop and tend to the wound, because they must keep moving. Moving despite the storm which threatens their existence—they cannot afford to look back. Because I am reigning with Christ, I am not my own.

It will cost me too much to look back. I'd rather endure the cross and despise the shame for an opportunity to sit down with God. Some people decide to take breaks from church and sit at home for long periods of time, while some never return. A soldier never takes breaks while in a war, he or she must keep fighting for their life and country. Hence, the moment we come to Christ we join the battle against good and evil, nonstop war until the enemy is destroyed. The cost for looking back, can be devastating. Sometimes we have devoted believers who are able to operate in the power of the Holy Spirit, heal the sick, cast out demons yet they succumb to the pressures of life and end up looking back—at that point the enemy takes over their lives. Matthew 12:43-45(KJV) says, "When the unclean spirit is gone out of a man, he walketh through dry places, seeking rest, and findeth none. Then he saith, I will return into my house from whence I came out; and when he is come, he findeth it empty, swept, and garnished. Then goeth he, and taketh with himself seven other spirits more wicked than himself, and they enter in and dwell there: and the last state of that man is worse than the first. Even so shall it be also unto this wicked generation. "These additional spirits come and take over your whole life, sexually, spiritually, emotionally, and financially. When these four areas are affected, it leaves you disorientated. That is why we cannot afford to look back. You find yourself wanting to have sex with everyone you see because another personality now lives in you. Spirits have personalities and whenever they live within a person that individual performs their acts. A person who is married finds it easy to cheat on their spouse with multiple partners yet finds no satisfaction. Ephesians 5:3-5 (KJV) tells us, "But fornication, and all uncleanness, or covetousness, let it not be once named among you, as becometh saints; Neither filthiness, nor foolish talking, nor jesting, which are not convenient: but rather giving of thanks. For this ye know, that no whoremonger, nor unclean person, nor covetous man, who is an idolater, hath any inheritance in the kingdom of Christ and of God." These are the characteristics of a soul which is controlled by demons.

When a believer is spiritually marred with demons, they know everything about God, they are unteachable, they are more spiritual than everyone else. They are always hearing from God and always have a revelation. When the spirit of religion finds its way in a person, it makes them feel high. The fall of King Saul is a prime example of how the spirit of religion can cause our demise, Saul thought he could sacrifice his way out. Samuel told him to wait seven days for him, yet he went ahead and made his own sacrifice. In those days only a man in the office of a priest could make a sacrifice. When these spirits live in you, they will fight for control over everything, even to take over the pastor's responsibilities.

Emotionally, when these spirits get into your soul, they make you operate from your feelings, rather than from your faith. They push you to do things out of the ordinary. Looking back will destroy the life the spirit of God created for you. That is one reason why many of our churches are so boring today, people are operating from their emotions and not from the spirit of God.

Financially, there seems to be a hole in your pocket. You never have money, as soon as you receive it, it goes. "By the sweat of your brow you will eat your food until you return to the ground, since from it you were taken; for dust you are and to dust you will return" Genesis 3:19 (NIV).

To break these personalities from your life you must first recognize that they are there in your soul and pray strategically against them. Meaning, you must focus on one area until God removes it from your life. Only you, God and the Holy Spirit can remove them, because their personalities are such a big part of you. 2 Corinthians 10:4-6(KJV):"For the weapons of our warfare *are* not carnal, but mighty through God to the pulling down of strongholds, casting down imaginations and every high thing that exalteth itself against the knowledge of God, and bringing into captivity every thought to the obedience of Christ, and having readiness to revenge all disobedience, when your obedience is fulfilled."

Many Christians have lost confidence in the things of God because of their lack of commitment and devotion. At times we get so busy, hardly making time for prayer and Bible study, neglecting to communicate with God. To reign with Christ, we must know who he is, grasp the gravity of what he has done for us and what it costed Jesus to purchase our redemption. If you do not know the price of something precious, you may take it for granted, but when you know how priceless the son of God really is, you will cherish his sacrifice every moment. If we truly plan on reigning with Christ, what will we look back to, what will we hold on to? Let us open our eyes and see the mess of this world and its fleeting pleasures, there is absolutely nothing to go back to once we have experienced Christ—do not be fooled.

Enduring Persecution for the Gospel's Sake

We often read the story of Cain and Abel, and the disciples of Jesus and we stand amazed. Not realizing that the same spirit is in our time and age. You will receive persecution for your faith from the world, including your family. We have heard so many stories of people who have been persecuted for their faith but in the end, they stood for God.

Kevin's older brother refused to work with him on the same job because he was a Christian. His brother did not want anything to do with God. He went to the superior requesting that his brother be transferred because he spoke too much of God. During this conflict, he kept on trusting God, to save his brother. One day while Kevin was singing the power of the Lord came in the room and touched his brother, just before he was transferred. His brother later told him that the spirit of the Lord came upon him and he felt like shouting, God had moved his heart to worship. Not long after he surrendered his life to the Lord. Kevin refused to be a Christian who does not share his faith with a world that is dying from sin. Even if it costs us our life and relationships, we must share the gospel with the world even when they do not want to hear it. Kevin was created and transformed to be salt and light, and his brother could not handle that. He wanted the world, but Kevin was determined to follow Jesus all the way, come what may, his mind was made up to go through the fire with Christ. He lost that job because of how the devil worked through his brother's complaint and was unemployed for three months. When he did get another job he struggled to keep it, the jobs were laced with nepotism and largely depended on who you knew. The employees were in cliques, represented by families and close friends; you were either a relative of theirs or you were considered a stranger. As you could imagine, this made the workplace uncomfortable, yet he clung to the word of God, and lived out his faith in front of them. One day Kevin's new supervisor called him to pray in remembrance of 9/11 with over eighty employees present that day. From that day on he became the man of prayer for them. During it all the Lord kept leading him to the Bible, it was through his word that he was assured of his protection and provision. He was determined to honor God with his life so that he could reign in him. What kind of believer are we if we do not want our friends and acquaintances to know of God? Jesus said in John 16:33 (KJV),"These things I have spoken unto you, that in me ye might have peace. In the world ye shall have tribulation: but be of good cheer, I have overcome the world."

Some of us believe that because we are Christians no ill or destruction will befall us, but Christ received persecution, so what about us? We cannot control the will of man, the heart of man is wicked, and they do as they please, so we will occasionally end up in their crosshairs. But we must believe that our God is faithful, and his purpose, protection and provision may come in several forms, whether through the closing of a door or his peace so that we may be of good cheer. Psalm 138:7 (KJV) says, "Though I walk in the midst of trouble, thou wilt revive me: thou shalt stretch forth thine hand against the wrath of mine enemies, and thy right hand shall save me."

To reign with Christ, you must be faithful at all costs, Jesus was faithful to God at all costs even to death. He had many opportunities to abandon his mission, but instead he denied himself, took up the cross and followed God's will for his life. If you look at the journey instead of the cause and the effect, you might give up! That is why God never shows us the journey, only the outcome. Therefore, to reign with Christ you must always keep the cause and the effect in view. Nothing is greater than your outcome. When we see the results at the end of the test, we will recognize that what we went through was worth it.

Forgiving Others

Another very important area we must all look out for is the sin of unforgiveness. If you allow it to grow it will paralyze your spiritual life and restrain you from fulfilling God's purpose for your life. Why should we allow the enemy of our soul to rob us of the privilege to approach God with a sincere heart? As Christians we should understand that God does not overlook the sin of unforgiveness. Therefore, at all times we should examine our lives before making requests of God. With all things considered, how long are you going to allow the devil to deceive you in believing that God is hearing your payer? Let me tell you this, he is not hearing you. Psalm 66:18(KJV) says, "If I regard iniquity in my heart, the Lord will not hear me." Regarding iniquity in heart means to keep a sin in one's heart and mind, unwilling to part ways with it. Such a sin is presumptuous, we consciously know something is sin and yet continue to cherish it. It is wickedness in conduct and appearance because we pretend that all is well with God and in our hearts. But newsflash, we are far from being perfect or right with God. The apostle Paul encourages us in 1 Corinthians 11:31(KJV):"For if we would judge ourselves, we should not be judged."

Kevin could have chosen to be bitter with his brother and former co-workers, but his obedience to the word of God to forgive and love was more important. Some of you have had to endure worse from family members and friends, but we have been called to grace and we should also offer grace.

Unforgiveness keeps us in bondage and out of the presence of God, it becomes a chain around our necks that takes us to unfamiliar places. It will make you dark and bitter, blocking your view of God, all you can see is the person who hurt you even when you go down to pray. Unforgiveness will exalt a person in your heart, so much so that the bitterness becomes a god, displacing the position of God. Whatever is on your mind other than God is a god to you, and that is sin. Jesus tells us to live in the spirit of forgiveness by forgiving those who hurt us. Sometimes the devil uses people who you love and trust the most to hurt you, to break, and frustrate your purpose in life. That is what he is after, to make you useless to God. The fact is, God cannot use you when you are bitter, because bitterness spreads easily and smears others to the advantage of the devil.

In contrast, forgiveness frees us from the weight of sin and gives us wings to fly into the presence of God. Forgiveness is grace which many have not mastered, and so Satan uses it to defeat people who are not willing to forgive. Matthew 5:23-24(KJV) says, "Therefore, if thou bring thy gift to the altar, and there rememberest that thy brother hath ought against thee; Leave there thy gift before the altar and go thy way; first be reconciled to thy brother, and then come and offer thy gift."

Unforgiveness not only separates us from God, it causes sickness and heart diseases. I am not saying that all sicknesses or diseases are a result of unforgiveness, but it is a possible cause. Therefore, as believers our responsibility is to free ourselves from malice, so that the healing power of the Lord can work in us and make us well.

Suffering with Christ

To reign with Christ, you must suffer with him, there is no escaping it. Acts 14:22(KJV) tells us,"…we must through much tribulation enter into the kingdom of God." When you have passed through your own fiery trials and found God to be true to what he says, you are better able to minister to, and help others. You have firsthand experience of both his sustaining grace and his purposeful design. You have a testimony of how he kept you through pain and how he reshaped you more into his image. What you experience from God, you can give away in increasing measure to others. The experiences given by God help us to develop the tenderness and charity necessary to help sanctify another person, especially in their deepest distress.

I had to learn this truth in 2 Timothy 2:12 (KJV), "If we suffer, we shall also reign with him: if we deny him, he also will deny us." Suffering helps to shape us into God's image. Think about a sculptor carving a sculpture, he uses shapes, clay, stone, marble, wood, and other materials to mold at his will. Sometimes these materials crack or break under the pressure but he does not give up, he tries again until he sees the final product. On this Christian journey we are going to experience suffering unlike nothing we have encountered, but the Holy Spirit will help us along the way. It does not matter how dark it gets; he will never leave us.

We often try to run from trials by giving God less of our time, shying away from prayer and fasting. Usually, the more we pray the more the devil attacks us. These amplified attacks are because he does not want us to get to where God wants us to be in him. Nevertheless, trials are tools God uses to bring us closer to him—it is the processing of the soul. When Kevin's brother and the foreman decided that they did not want him around, he did not give up on God, in fact it drew him closer to the Lord. Not only did he learn that men will fail, but your own family can. He turned his attention toward the Lord even more. If the devil sees that these things get you down easily, he will continue to bombard your life with them, and sooner or later you will become weary and drained or may even fall in depression. To think that the persons who should have your back are the ones pulling you down and despising you, is more than what one person should bear. Remind yourself that Christ went through worse for our sins. Isaiah 53:3 (KJV) says, "He is despised and rejected of men; a man of sorrows and acquainted with grief: and we hid as it were our faces from him; he was despised, and we esteemed him not."

God's purpose is always greater than what we see, and we have a tendency of looking at the problem instead of the outcome. That is why if we are not mindful, we take it personally, when it really is not. While Satan wants us to take it personally so that he can defeat God's plan for our lives, he knows that it is not about us. We are the tools God chose to use for his glory and if the devil can take our minds off what really matters, we cannot reign with Christ.

That is why it is very important to draw strength from the Lord daily, so that you can stand when evil comes against you. There were times when it seemed like my entire family was against me, there was no one to talk to when things got rough. You must build your life on Christ alone, not on family and friends but on Christ alone. When you are pursuing God, the devil will use anything to discourage you, especially those closest to you. He wants you to be bitter with them, so that you will miss God's plan for your life. He also knows that they will come to know Christ because of you and his plan is to stop them from coming to God. Therefore, we must ignore the process and focus on Christ.

When Babylon rose against Israel and took thousands captive, God allowed it because they had turn away from him, and instead of giving up on them he put them in the refiner's fire to save them. God is not out to destroy his people and as such he allows circumstances to bring us to him. 2 Chronicles 7:13-14 (KJV) reads, "If I shut up heaven that there be no rain, or if I command the locusts to devour the land, or if I send pestilence among my people; If my people, which are called by my name, shall humble themselves, and pray, and seek my face, and turn from their wicked ways; then will I hear from heaven, and will forgive their sin, and will heal their land."

The problem with many believers today is that we want to be problem free without putting in the work. We expect God to do all the work while we walk free. To reign with Christ takes sacrifice and devotion on our part, all he asks us to do is to pray and trust him, Philippians 2:12 (KJV) says, "Wherefore, my beloved, as ye have always obeyed, not as in my presence only, but now much more in my absence, work out your own salvation with fear and trembling."

When the apostle Paul was stoned by an angry mob after preaching the gospel and was dragged out of the city and left for dead, he did not ask God, "Why me?" because he understood the words of Jesus in John 15:20-21 (KJV),which say, "Remember the word that I said unto you, the servant is not greater than his lord. If they have persecuted me, they will also persecute you; if they have kept my saying, they will keep yours also. But all these things will they do unto you for my name's sake, because they know not him that sent me." Some might have asked God why He allowed that to happen to a man who was obeying Jesus' command to preach the gospel, but we must remember and believe that God is perfect in all is ways.

When the Kentucky county clerk was put in prison for not signing a same-sex marriage license, some probably questioned if God is as strong as he claims to be. Sometimes we expect God to change things immediately, but God does not think like man. Proverbs 28:1 (KJV) tells us that "The wicked flee when no one pursueth, but the righteous are bold as a lion." God has a time when he will say enough is enough, while we are waiting, he expects us to stand for righteousness even if it is going to cost us our lives.

I believe that many believers today including myself, are questioning God. We claim with our words that we do not question him, but our actions prove otherwise. We are not sure if we can trust him, seeing how today Christian principles are mocked and even Christians themselves are persecuted and beheaded. It would appear God that we are losing the fight. The fact is some believers are not doing what they are called to do and as a result the devil gets the upper hand in their lives and society at large. We are called to trust and obey God's instructions and to walk in the spirit, failure to do so leads to unbelief as well as unproductivity. First, most of us fail to proclaim who Jesus is or we do not know who he is. If this is the case, then there is a need to know who Jesus is. When a believer gets to that place in their walk with Christ, they will not question God, because his will becomes theirs and they crave to please him no matter what.

Our Christian principles are mocked simply because of false believers and false proclaimers who have watered down the word of God, preaching themselves rather than Christ who was crucified. When people water down the message it is because they want to be accepted by everyone or they are without a message from God. To get a message from the Lord you must have a relationship with him, otherwise your message will have no influence or impact on society. Society on a whole is looking for hope that is found only in Christ and proclaimers of the gospel are given the responsibility to proclaim and to demonstrate the power of God. We have seen through the ages that many have lost their lives for proclaiming Christ and for standing on the side of righteousness. There are many reasons why Christians are persecuted, sometimes religion may be tied to ethnic or cultural identity. In other places, governments who thrive on power view Jesus as a competition and those who follow him as threats. Still, in some regions a high value is put on their major religion, so much so that any other faith is seen as something to be rooted out and violently oppressed. These are only a few reasons why Christians must be true soldiers of the cross of Christ. We cannot be silent because of persecution and suffering.

Desiring the Will of God for Our Lives

His plans for us are far greater than our imagination. Joseph was his father's favorite son among the twelve sons. His brothers hated him and ended up selling him because of his dreams and aspirations. Joseph thought he would merely be the leader of the family because of his dream, but God had a bigger plan for him. If your plan is only for your family, you do not have a big enough plan. God's plan for us is to bless everyone in the world, not to limit it to one's race or one's family but to extend it to all mankind.

It is selfish to expect God to bless us and not others, as though we are the only ones who need blessings. Jesus teaches us to love our neighbors as we love ourselves; I should desire the same things for you and your children as I do for myself. But Joseph's brothers wanted to kill him rather than to see his dreams come to pass.

So many church leaders have hindered their members from becoming someone great in God's kingdom out of jealousy. These malicious practices do not hold back the believer, but they interfere with the will and move of God and these evil works will be judged.

I have seen a pastor overlook his young armor bearer who he mentored for years for pastoral duties when he retired. While in active duty the pastor would allow this anointed man of God to preach when he was unable to, but he passed him up for the pastoral role and gave it to his friend instead. The friend was on fire for God until the pastor died, after his death the church stopped growing and he lost fervor. All this time the young armor bearer continued to grow in his walk with God, full of passion for the work of the Kingdom. Sometimes leaders allow their fleshly ideals to block the purpose of God. They ignore the will of God because by their standards qualifications are not met.

Joseph went through a terrible ordeal to get to where God wanted him to be; from being sold as a slave, to becoming a housekeeper, to being falsely accused by his master's wife because he refused to sleep with her and was subsequently sentenced to prison. Even in prison his calling of leadership was apparent, since he rose to become the supervisor. He was effective and established irrespective of what he was subjected to. This was because God was with Joseph and he was using his assumed tribulations to develop his character for the position as second ruler in Egypt (see Genesis 41:42-46). All through this, Joseph honored God and never rejected his will.

God's will for our lives often requires us submitting our fears, our own efforts and our own desires to his sovereignty. This can be difficult and unappealing since God's will can also take time. However, our commitment and our obedience to his word and his leading should be more important to us than us gaining instant gratification.

Irrespective of what we will face, we must remember that God loves us. He is our caring Father, and he has a plan for us far beyond what we can see for ourselves. Christ offered himself for us, every human being is under his watchful eye, he cares for all of us and he watches over us with compassion. As parents naturally care for their children, God supernaturally cares for each of us. He knows everything about us and feels our pain. When one of his creation hurts, he too feels that pain and when we hurt each other we break His heart since we are not walking in truth. We must die to our will and seek to please God and only him.

CHAPTER THREE
Living in Christ

As we live in Christ we are expected to walk in authority. Once we have died to our old ways and the flesh, true living begins in God. To reign with Christ, you must abide in him. According to the Merriam-Webster Dictionary to abide means to remain stable or fixed in a state. John 15:4-5 (KJV) says, "Abide in me, and I in you. As the branch cannot bear fruit of itself, except it abide in the vine; no more can ye, except ye abide in me. I am the vine, ye are the branches: He that abideth in me, and I in him, the same bringeth forth much fruit: for without me ye can do nothing." The Lord wants us to live our lives in him. To overcome the world, we must abide in Christ, there is no other way to overcome the world. It is impossible to overcome the world without the Lord, no matter how clever you are. We ought to stay fixed in our pursuit of God and the things of the Kingdom. Although we will wrestle with sin and be persecuted by others, experience suffering and disappointments in this life, God wants us to live full lives. He wants us to be bountiful and overflowing with joy, grace and goodness, each day we are awake.

Living by Faith
It is by faith we follow God. Hebrews 11:6 (KJV) says, "But without faith it is impossible to please him: for he that cometh to God must believe that he is, and that he is a rewarder of them that diligently seek him." Faith is believing in God without seeing the evidence of what we have prayed for, yet we know that God cannot fail and will not fail.

God's will for us is a life of faith, not knowing where the money is coming from to pay the bills, yet we believe it is coming before the due date. Living by faith is not new, Abraham the father of faith believed God when he told him to leave his country and his father's house to journey to a land he had never been before. Abraham obeyed God not knowing where he was going, nevertheless, his faith was unshakable in his God. We too must take the leap and go out by faith for our ministries, our country, our healing, our finances, and our families. Whatever stands before you, bring it to God by faith.

To reign with Christ, we must willingly follow him not just in words but thoughts and actions. People will easily follow you when things are going well because they see where you are headed, and it looks promising, and they have something to gain from it. They will put you on the highest seat, but as soon as it gets dark, they forget their promises. "And he said unto him, Lord, I am ready to go with thee, both into prison, and to death," see Luke 22:33 (KJV). Peter was willing to go with Jesus in words but not in action. Subsequently, he denied Jesus three times, saying, "I don't know the man!" Matthew 26:72 (NIV).

Many are saying, "Lord, I will die for you"; God does not want us to die for him. He has nothing to gain from our deaths, that is why he died for us. Christ wants us to follow him through life by faith and through death to sin by faith, for it is only through death to sin that we bring God glory. The apostle Paul understood this when he declared in Galatians 2:20 (KJV), "I am crucified with Christ: nevertheless, I live; yet not I, but Christ lives in me: and the life which I now live in the flesh I live by the faith of the Son of God, who loved me, and gave himself for me." The things that prevent us from becoming one with him are the things God wants to kill in our lives.

It was easy for Peter to follow Christ because he was there with him, but when the time came for Christ to be taken away from him, he denied him. In my own ministry as a young pastor many people promised, "Pastor, I am going to stay with your ministry because you are a wonderful man of God." But when the dust settled, they were nowhere to be found. Their intentions were good, but their willingness was out of line with God.

When our hearts are purified the fire of God will consume the sacrifice that we bring to him. When Peter received the Holy Spirit, he was ready to go through death with him, he preached the gospel without fear. Jerusalem and the rest of the world was afraid of them because the risen Lord was working through them by his power. When he finished the work that Christ gave him to do, the Roman Empire decided to execute him by crucifixion. He requested to be crucified upside down, since he felt he was not worthy to die the way the Lord did. But he was willing to follow Christ through death. It is by fellowshipping with Christ we reign with him, not by how educated we are nor by how efficiently we speak, but by the relationship we have with him.

Aligning Our Personal Desires

The importance of one's personal desires must not be ignored. Many wonder if they can really be the kind of person who God wants them to be. The real concern should be "Do I desire to be the kind of person God wants me to be?" We often make our paths for a career, to become a doctor, lawyer, nurse, teacher, or governor. We think pushing our careers and self-development is noble, which is completely fine since we live in the temporal and need to survive, but what about our desire for the things of God? Are we as concerned about them as we are about other things? Paul spoke of the "…yea, what vehement desire, yea, what zeal" the Corinthians had in carrying out the instructions concerning their personal problems which he had addressed in his first letter to the Corinthians (see 2 Corinthians 7:7-11 KJV), their desire for spiritual wholeness enabled them to overcome their spiritual deficiencies.

We should constantly desire to reflect the character of God; we should chart courses and design vision boards to God in our spiritual walk. Do we challenge ourselves to read the Bible more, to know scripture, to evangelize more? Do we spend our money on tuition for Bible school or to buy kingdom books to aid in our personal Bible study? We ought to pursue the things of God earnestly and intentionally for our spiritual growth which needs nurturing and daily sculpting. "Blessed are those who hunger and thirst for righteousness, for they shall be filled," says Matthew 5:6 (NIV).

Unfortunately, some people only chase God to fix their problems and after the problem is solved God is out of their lives because they only needed a problem solver not a father, when a father is there forever. Problem solvers come and go. Some family members only call when they need help and outside of that they neglect to stay in touch. This can be distasteful and will run one's patience thin since you are only seen as a convenience. Do not take God for convenience, if you do, one day you will regret it. Proverbs 1:24 (KJV) reads, "Because I have called, and ye refused; I have stretched out my hand, and no man regarded."

You must be a God chaser, to chase God means to seek to dwell in his presence, wisdom, and knowledge, with the ability to hear his voice and know his will and desire his ways. Wanting God should be second nature just like the air you breathe because you cannot live without it. Similarly, we cannot live without God. Day and night our souls should crave his presence. When was the last time you had a sleepless night because you spent it seeking his face? Not because you want something from him but because you want him. When was the last time you heard the voice of the Lord? Psalm 42:1-2 (KJV) says, "As the hart panteth after the water brooks, so panteth my soul after thee, O God. My soul thirsteth for God, for the living God: when shall I come and appear before God?" There must always be a longing for God in the life of believers because he is our source of life, the rock on which we stand, our compass in the time of storm, our bridge over troubled water and the anchor for our souls.

It breaks the heart of God when we ignore his presence and refuse to obey his will for our lives. In so doing we miss out on so much of what he wants to share with us.

God Wants Us to Win in Life

To win means to succeed, overcome adversity and live a conquering life. Everyone wants to triumph in life or to get ahead. Life can be challenging without someone to help you or guide you through it. It is usually easier when we have someone older or more advanced guiding us, who has already experienced what we are going through and has successfully navigated that phase of life. Their guidance can help us to the top faster than anyone else can or even on our own. A young man started his own business without guidance or supervision, as time progressed customers would come asking for credit until their pay day, he saw profitability in the idea and he had good returns. He decided to expand his business and hired employees, he then decided to stay at home since the business could sustain itself. After a while he realized that his business was failing, he had more customers than before, but less money was coming in which forced him to close his business. He was not around to keep customers accountable, and his employees were not as dedicated to his business and vision.

When you stand alone the devil will force you out of business. He will create circumstances which will push you over the cliff. He does not want you to proper or to win in life, his only desire is to see you fall. Therefore, God has given us a defense system to win.

To prosper is the condition of being successful. The devil is like a raging bull, annoyed whenever He sees the children of God thriving. When Satan saw the prosperity of Job, he was mad, but could not touch him, because God protected him on every side. Job 1:8-10 (KJV)says, "And the Lord said unto Satan, hast thou considered my servant Job, that there is none like him in the earth, a perfect and an upright man, one that feared God, and eschewed evil? Then Satan answered the Lord, and said, Doth Job fear God for naught? Hast not thou made a hedge about him, and about his house, and about all that he hath on every side? Thou hast blessed the work of his hands, and his substance is increased in the land."

Those who reign with Christ win in life; this is our inheritance after becoming born again. Jesus came in the form of flesh as the son of God to show us the Father. The most compelling argument for Christ's authority comes from his birth, death, resurrection, and ascension. Never was it heard or conceived by anyone that God had a biological son, while many are called children of God, qualified simply by their belief in God. Despite all the evidence in the Bible supporting his coming into the world from Genesis through Revelation, most men refuse to acknowledge the one true God. The hardness of man's heart outweighs his faith to believe that it is possible for God to become man. If we cannot believe that Christ is the son of God, then we are not worthy of heaven or the son of God. If we do not believe that Christ is the son of God and all authority is given unto him, we cannot reign on earth in him.

God can have us sit with him in heavenly places while we are on earth because we are in Christ, who dwells in heaven. Christ is seated there because he won the victory over Satan and the host of hell. The church is in him enjoying a life of victory over the enemy. No matter what the devil brings against us, we have already won, because Christ defeated the devil by going to the cross and he took the power of death from him. We have already won in Christ and will continue to win. We will win in our relationships, in our businesses, in our ministries, in our walk with Christ. All we do will prosper, we will speak a thing and it will come forth.

Living in Joy

Joy is a feeling that cannot be bought, no matter how much you earn or what you have accomplished, you must receive and know that God has something good in store for you and it is he who gives all good gifts. You cannot believe he intends for you to live a life of painful labor in which each day is a total struggle. The Bible talks about the joy of the Lord being our strength, it offers many examples of God wanting us to have joy. This does not mean we are only going to see stars and rainbows, but the joy of the Lord should constantly be felt in our hearts.

In Psalm 63:7 (ESV), David said, "...for you have been my help, and in the shadow of your wings I will sing for joy." I sing whenever I feel the presence of the Lord, and sometimes I just shout because having God makes me happy. Some mornings when I turn the tap on to brush my teeth and wash my face, I hear a choir on the inside of my heart singing. If you are always unhappy and weighed down, then something is wrong. You are either not doing what you were called to be doing or in a position you have outgrown, and God has revealed it to you. Life is challenging, and there will be times when we are bogged down, but that should not be our constant state. We should be full of joy at work, in our relationships, in our ministries, in our recreational time and most importantly in our walk with God.

Whenever my brother is faced with something beyond his control the Lord always sends me to pray for him. Despite what is going on in the family I was willing to follow the Lord's instructions and many times the Lord speared him. He once told my sister that if it were not for me praying for him, he would have been killed. Never allow discouragement to stop you from doing the Lord's will or allow bitterness to spring in your heart because of your family—instead, love them unconditionally. Sometimes your disobedience could be what causes your brother's sorrow to continue. We have been created for fellowship and if you are able to brighten someone's day, do it. However, our joy should not be external; it should not be dependent on people nor what we have. We should be joyful because it is a fruit of the spirit, because the spirit of God lives in us. If that is not reflected in our lives, we should seek God for it earnestly. If we allow ourselves to wallow in sorrow, unhappiness, and dread, this suggests that we do not know God. This suggests that we are not reigning in God, acknowledging his authority to fix our lives, calm our seas and make a way.

Get Off the Fence

Some born-again believers are still conflicted with whether they want to be serving God. When their husband is being loving and providing for the home, they want to be submissive and respectful wives, but when the man becomes neglectful and is laid off, they want to commit adultery. There are some young Christians who are hot and willing to facilitate youth camps and serve on a Sunday, but when Jay-Z is headlining at a concert nearby, church service is put on hold. There are also church members who actively and religiously participate in gambling. Some of us need to get off the fence and pick a side!

A fence is a line between two lands, it does not belong to any one but stands as a divider on the border of both lands. Unfortunately, many of God's people are like a fence, standing between God and the world but belonging to neither. Anyone can jump that fence or tear it down because it does not represent either side, but only stands as the middleman. To reign with Christ, we must stand for him. It must be clear to the world whose we are and what we stand for.

Religion is a fence for many, and indeed it sometimes keeps us from knowing God because it is filled with human error and doctrine that neither take us to God nor away from him but keeps us in the middle. This kind of lifestyle infuriates God. Matthew 23:1-4(KJV) reads, "Then spake Jesus to the multitude, and to his disciples, saying the scribes and the Pharisees sit in Moses' seat: All therefore whatsoever they bid you observe, that observe and do; but do not ye after their works: for they say, and do not. For they bind heavy burdens and grievous to be borne and lay them on men's shoulders; but they themselves will not move them with one of their fingers."

Man's doctrine only gives you an awareness of God, but not the knowledge of him. The knowledge of God can only be found by seeking his face in prayer and fasting. When Jesus was baptized the Holy Spirit came upon him and led him into the wilderness on fasting for four days and nights to make him ready for the mission he came to accomplish. Knowledge is power, and the more knowledge you have of God the more power you have in him. "My people are destroyed for lack of knowledge: because thou hast rejected knowledge, I will also reject thee, that thou shalt be no priest to me: seeing thou hast forgotten the law of thy God, I will also forget thy children," says Hosea 4: 6 (KJV).

If you want the blessing of God, you must get off the fence and choose a side, you cannot have God and the world. Furthermore, you are accountable for the fact that there is a God who loves you unconditionally and redeems us with his blood. You can make all the excuses you want; God holds you accountable for the nails in his hands and for the crown of thorns on his head. God holds the world accountable for the blood of Jesus Christ, we cannot take it for granted. See Isaiah 53:3-7, which speaks of how Jesus would be rejected and despised by man.

Fence Christians are not Christians, they are caught up in their own world and cannot bring glory to God. A young man in the church fell in love with one of the sisters, and they started dating. After dating for a while, they decided that they were compatible for each other, but the young man told her that he wanted to have sex before marriage. She told him no, she refused to dishonor God. He left the relationship, found someone else who was willing to dishonor God, married her, but two years later they got a divorce. A believer who is living for Christ cannot be sitting on the fence. Matter of fact, I think the path of the "fence Christian" is harder than that of a believer who is completely sold out to Christ. God is looking for people who are willing to stand up for him even if it is going to cost them everything. The church sister was willing to say no and stood with God rather than to engage in fornication and dishonor God and herself. Some people are indulging in this kind of lifestyle and expect God to bless their marriages. God cannot and will not bless sin, that is one reason why we have so many divorces among believers today. God is not in these kinds of marriages. 1 Corinthians 6:9-10 (KJV) says, "Know ye not that the unrighteous shall not inherit the kingdom of God? Be not deceived: neither fornicators, nor idolaters, nor adulterers, nor effeminate, nor abusers of themselves with mankind, nor thieves, nor covetous, nor drunkards, nor revilers, nor extortioners, shall inherit the kingdom of God."

If you are on the fence, get off quickly while there is time, ask the Lord to forgive you and turn from sin. He loves you with an everlasting love and is not willing that you would perish in any way.

Living Boldly through the Holy Spirit

To reign with Christ, you must have the Holy Spirit, if you do not have him you are not qualified as a child of God. I have spoken about the Holy Spirit in other chapters, but his value in our lives is all encompassing. His presence in our lives helps us in all areas, whether it is dying to the flesh or living victoriously daily. Believers often become ignorant of right and wrong when they want to do their own thing. When they want to get away with indulging in a particular sin they start questioning what the scriptures said, even enquiring of the scriptures from believers who are more liberal and who would entertain what they want to do. But when we have the Holy Spirit, we do not need to ask anyone about what is right or wrong, he will convict us of sin, guiding us into righteous living. We run the risk of being led away and deceived when we listen to the voice of liberal men, but the voice of the Holy Spirit, being the good shepherd is able to keep us from falling away. The Holy Spirit is our banner and our boldness to walk out our faith in this world. The world is filled with wickedness and therefore the Holy Spirit came to guide and help us into all truth. To have him you must first receive Christ, the moment that you accept Christ as your Lord and savior the Holy Spirit comes and dwells in you. To receive the Holy Spirit, you must first know who He is. He is God, restored to man in his Spirit. Therefore, when we approach him, we should do so with reverence, respect, and worship. When Jesus purchased our redemption, it speaks of being owned by him, as such we are restored to him when we receive Christ as Lord and savior. Not by might, nor by power, but by my spirit, saith the Lord of hosts, Zechariah 4:6 KJV.

Furthermore, to receive the power of the Holy Spirit you must be ready to work. Jesus did not receive the Holy Spirit until he was ready to work. To live boldly and effectively in this life, we must acknowledge and rely on the Holy Spirit. Therefore, I cannot stress the importance of the Holy Spirit enough.

Supporting Those with a Calling

In every saved family there is usually one who is more committed to the Lord, this person ends up reigning greatly in Christ while on earth. It is very important to understand and recognize the Joseph, Esther, or David in your family. We have grown to celebrate those Biblical stalwarts but in our own families we struggle to accept them. Many families are missing out on their greatest blessing because the one God chose is less esteemed within the family. God does not look at the outward appearance of men, but he looks at the heart.

God sent Jesus to call at least one from every family and to bring him or her into his family through the blood of Jesus. That one becomes responsible for the spiritual sensitivities of the family towards God, until the whole family comes to Christ. It is paramount that you do not despise the one God has chosen to lead the family to him. You might be in a better position financially, academically, and are more preferred by everyone around you, but that does not automatically qualify you as the tool God wants to use. A person who depends on his or herself is not the kind of person God can use to bring his glory, but he requires a person who depends on him for help.

God chose Joseph because he was not self-centered but God-centered. When a man or woman is self-centered, they become easy prey for the devil. They will do and say anything just to be seen and heard going out of their way to be recognized by others, such a person is an instrument for the works of darkness. It is almost impossible to lead a person who trusts in himself, if he cannot see the outcome, he will not move or do what God says to do. Since it is always about him he has to see it before he can believe it, and that is a poor candidate for the kingdom. God is looking for people who will go out on the limb for him by just loving him. Hebrews 11:4-6 (KJV) tells us, "By faith Abel offered to God a better sacrifice than Cain, by which he obtained the testimony that he was righteous, God testifying about his gifts, and through faith, though he is dead, he still speaks. By faith Enoch was taken up so that he should not see death; and he was not found because God took him up; for he obtained the witness that before his being taken up he was pleasing to God. And without faith it is impossible to please Him, for he who comes to God must believe that He is, and that He is a rewarder of those who seek Him."

Because of Joseph's God-centered lifestyle, God showed him the end from the beginning, and he had faith in what he saw. His brothers could not understand why God would choose him and not them, why they would come and bow down to him. When God is in you all things are possible. Our life in Christendom is not a one man show, the Bible speaks about all members of the body working together and our desires as believers should be for our families to be saved and for our friends to come to know God.

Knowing Christ and Making Him Known

Let us not forget that we were commissioned to preach the gospel to all nations. There is a Jamaican proverb which says, learn to dance at home before going abroad. We ought to be ministers in our homes first and foremost, with as much urgency and energy as we extend outside. I grew up in a home with parents who loved the Lord and were willing to live for him. As such, I received a solid spiritual foundation which has stood firm even into adulthood. I cherish the work they did to cultivate sound spiritual habits. They lived surrendered lives to the Lord which was evident to all who knew them including myself. Their lifestyle opened my understanding to what it means to serve God in spirit and truth. Today these kinds of examples are very hard to find, mainly because people have become self-centered. They are more focused on what they want to achieve and to own, rather than on God who is the giver of all things. I remember every Sunday morning at 5 A.M. our parents would wake us up for prayer and all of us had to pray. Some of us were still sleeping but we had to be there. They instilled a culture of prayer; those were the years of training in the way we should go. Today we let our children tell us what to do, when and if they are going to church, as a result we have a generation that does not know God. Church was not the first place I was taught about God; my parents were the ones who taught me to love the Lord and to follow him. I was discipled from the comfort of my home, by my parents. As Christians we have the responsibility of teaching our children and others about God, his grace, and mercies. This is our commission, to make disciples of all nations (see Matthew 28:19) and where better to start than in our own homes and bloodline? We should let our lights shine before our parents, our children, our friends, and our employers, that they may come to know Christ.

Knowing God is more than our church attendance. I would imagine that the Lord won't be in heaven with the church register, recalling our weekly visits or lack thereof. A church sister fell ill to the point of death and in those moments her prayer to God was to remind him about her journey in church. She recounted her days growing up in church and how she maintained active participation while in college. She got engaged and later married, yet she remained in the church and was raising her children in like manner. After she was done, the Lord told her how attending church was not enough to get her into heaven. She had to be born again, just as how a baby is born into a family and is groomed by them, she needed to be born again in his family. She found this hard to comprehend so she reasoned with God on how she believed she had all the prerequisites. But he asked her, do you know me? Many of us religiously attend church but do we know Jesus? Do we know him and the power of his resurrection? Do we share his sufferings becoming like him in his death? (see Philippians 3:10-11). Apart from listening to sermons from our Pastors on a Sunday, do we have a personal walk with him?

Christ had compassion on her because she ignorantly believed that she knew him; and he healed her. Her encounter with Christ changed her life forever. It is so easy to talk about people without knowing them, we base our conversations on what we heard about them from someone else or we judge them based on their appearance. But in the Kingdom, active and deep pursuit is required, surface worship and communion simply will not cut it. When you know Christ, your life reflects his life and his glory; so much so that others can see and feel his presence with and in you. My dear friends, there are people just like you and me who have spent their whole lives in church and at the end of their lives they find no rest for their souls; let that not be us.

When we know Christ, it should be our desire to have others know him, especially those in our families. We should intercede for the salvation of those we interact with daily, sharing the good news of our live hope. A man told is father that he did not believe in God, heaven, nor hell, because of his exposure to theories put forward by researchers on the world's creation and attempts to discredit miracles in the Bible. He was further dissuaded because of the evil of today. But his father continued to pray that one day his son would come to know the Lord as his savior and Lord. The father died without seeing his prayer answered. As the Lord ordained it, an elderly lady went to the community where the son lived and held a revival service. The son's wife begged him to accompany her, and he reluctantly went. That night the preacher preached on the subject 'Where will you spend eternity.' Immediately the Holy Spirit opened his eyes and he saw himself in hell crying for help but there was no one to help. He heard the voice of his father praying for him, "Lord, have Mercy on my son," that night he surrendered his life to the Lord. It may be your own son, daughter, or a family member, who the devil is using to challenge your faith in this way. Do not give up, keep on praying, one day God will have mercy and give a heart of flesh where it was once stony.

Manifesting His Glory

If we are living in the presence of God, full of the Holy Spirit and following Christ's examples, we should be operating in his glory. One of the manifestations of his glory on earth is the ability to heal the sick and perform other miracles. Yes, we should constantly be experiencing miracles, we were told that we would do greater works than what Jesus did.

To heal the sick means to make healthy, sound, and free from ailment, by the power of the Holy Spirit—he is the remedy for every sickness. He created all things and therefore has the answer for everything. Believers have the responsibility to administer the solution of the Holy spirit, through the resources he as provided such a preaching, teaching, worshiping, counseling, evangelism, sharing of our substances like clothes and food with those in need. These are just a few of the vast number of resources available for us to work with.

People all over the world are experiencing all kinds of illnesses which doctors have no cure for. While scientists are working tirelessly to come up with the answers to solve human problems especially of sicknesses and diseases, they often look to technology and human wisdom to find the answers. When the Holy Spirit cures you from a sickness, it never repeats itself because He goes beyond science to the core of the problem. While God gave man wisdom to heal the sick by way of technology and medication, there are sicknesses that only God can cure. Yet men seem to depend on man rather than God, because they are not willing to exercise their faith in God, and therefore suffer greatly. It is never the doctors who heal us from sicknesses, but always the work of the Holy Spirit. As such, believers hath to trust God for healing even when they must see the doctor, because he is the great physician who heals the sick, he is the sympathizing Jesus.

Years before my mother died, she fell ill, upon examining her the doctor told my father that there was nothing he could do. He told my father that we should prepare for her death. When my father looked on his thirteen children who needed their mother, he was greatly moved, and he called the church to prayer and fasting. The Lord showed up like he usually does, and he healed her.

Never doubt the power of the Holy Spirit and your ability to activate healing in yourself and others. Matthew 7:7-8 (KJV) says, "Ask, and it shall be given you; seek, and ye shall find; knock, and it shall be opened unto you: For every one that asked received; and he that seek find; and to him that knock it shall be opened." The life of the believer cannot be effective with doubt. Once doubt enters, it reduces our zeal and optimism. Doubt stops the hands of God from moving in our lives. When Jesus called Peter to walk on the water, he started out well, but he took his eyes off Jesus and he doubted. As he began to look at the waves which were coming towards him, immediately he started to sink. The best way to get things done or to see a miracle, is to believe that what you ask God for is granted. Kill the spirit of doubt and trust the Lord with all your heart.

The bountiful life of Christ cannot be kept secret or just in the inward workings but should be manifested and used to uplift the lives of others. We should spend time in prayer for our unbelief so that the glory of God can invade our lives.

CHAPTER FOUR
Enduring the War

In Chapter Two we spoke about dying with Christ, denying ourselves and enduring persecution from the world. But as much as we live in a temporal world, we contend with the spirit. A believer who does not accept nor believe this, is already defeated. It is easy for us to ignore the person at work who we know is against us, since if we keep out of their crosshairs, we might be fine. But the devil is out like a roaring lion, seeking whom he may devour (see 1 Peter 5:8 KJV). Ephesians 6:10-11 KJV says, "We ought to be strong in the Lord and the power of his might, that we should put on the whole armor of God that we might be able to stand against the schemes of the devil." We are soldiers and we are in a war.

Using the Word of God

The Bible is the word of God and is useful as instruction and guidance in righteousness, so that we as servants of God may be thoroughly equipped for every good work (see 2 Timothy 3:16-17 KJV). How can we then operate as Christians without our instruction manual? How can we effectively reign in Christendom if we are unequipped to do every good work? While we live on earth, we will be faced with challenges, trials, and warfare, but the word of God is our weapon. It is in the Bible that we find who we are, what is expected of us, whose we are and what God can and will do for us.

The books in the Bible have been referred to as the canon, as the spiritual authority for the Christian, full of truth and complete in its message. However, many persons doubt the completeness and accuracy of this message. But the Bible is one of the oldest literatures and though it has been displaced and translated its essence is closer to its original writings than any other book. While there are others who argue that based on the Bible God condones suffering, oppression, mass murder, discrimination; and some Christians have used it to do just that. It is ironic how holy some perceive themselves to be, to judge God when we are a generation quick to retaliate, to sue and to seek justice. Yet, we fail to see that God is a deliverer, a provider and a defender as highlighted in those very same scriptures. "The Lord is righteous in all his ways, and holy in all his works," says Psalm 145:17(KJV).

The fact is, the Bible shows man his sinful nature which may be off-putting for some to look at. What he thinks himself to be is less than his reality. When you do not want to change you will fight the change. A child who is sick from a cold or fever will put up a fight not to take medication because he or she does not know what is best for them, such is man. The word of God is like a mirror—it shows us our state, it shows us where we fall short by the standards of our Father. However, we must apply the word in the areas where we are failing, so as not to be only hearers of the word who walk away still misaligned, though we saw from the mirror that we need fixing.

"Anyone who listens to the word but does not do what it says is like someone who looks at his face in a mirror and, after looking at himself, goes away and immediately forgets what he looks like. But whoever looks intently into the perfect law that gives freedom, and continues in it, not forgetting what they have heard, but doing it they will be blessed in what they do," James 1:23-25(NIV).

Our aim as believers is to be more like Christ, which can only be done through reading and applying scriptures. "He that saith he abideth in him ought himself also to walk, even as he walked," see 1 John 2:6 (KJV).

We Are Expected to Pray

As believers we are expected to pray, to have deep communication and fellowship with God as often as we can. Prayer should be our lifeline, it should be our first line of defense, not our spouse, not our words, not our fists, not the secrets we know, not witchcraft, not our friends.

I love to pray and read my Bible because the results always present themselves whenever I present my case to the Lord. This was something I grew up seeing my parents do; they prayed and God answered. Those years of manifestation have made it easy for me to approach the Lord and ask for whatever I need. As I got older, I realized that they were demonstrating faith all those years and that faith produces trust in God. I encourage parents to build an altar in your homes, let your children see you pray and pray with them also. These practices will produce faith in them for years to come. Those years of intercession by my parents prepared me for what God is now doing in my life. Yes, I still went through many trials and oppression, but the devil could not kill me. He tried, but the seed of righteousness was already planted by my parents and the foundation for an altar of prayer was already laid.

On a regular day after my wife left for work and my children for school, I decided to fast; the Lord told me to send prayer via voicenote in my siblings WhatsApp group. As I prayed, I got a vision, I saw heaven open and souls ascending into heaven, angels surrounded the portal and I saw Jesus standing at the gate to let them in. Those who did not have his blood, nor the seal of the Holy Spirit were sent back. I saw hosts of souls going up to God, they were not in human form but were like the breath of God going up to their heavenly Father to reap their eternal rewards. "Then shall the dust return to the earth as it was: and the spirit shall return unto God who gave it," Ecclesiastes 12:7 (KJV). I saw myself taken up among the souls, and in that moment, I asked the Lord what they were, and he told me they were souls. I reached out my hands and touched a few, they felt soft and delicate. Jesus told me not to touch them because they were going to the Father where they would spend eternity with him. My garment was changed, and he gave me a rod with a sword inside the rod, and a compass on top of the rod pointing to the four corners of the earth in a ball made of glass. The rod was much taller than I was, but I was able to point it. My garment was black, with a protective shield so that nothing could penetrate it or harm me. God then said to me, "You will stand before the gods of the earth and preach and defend the gospel." Christ took me to the Father who was waiting for me. "Come up higher," He said to me. I was surrounded by much glory, power, love, peace, joy, and happiness; I had never felt such intensity before. His appearance was like crystals, he glistened.

I remember when I was a young man preaching on a train in New York City with many people on board, I saw the spirit of God in the same form on the train one day. After seeing him I had no fear, I became bold in my preaching. The people became quiet as they listened to the word of God. I knew immediately he was the Holy Spirit, and He was the same Spirit of God speaking to me in my vision. He brought me through another portal of heaven and showed me many high mountains and his presence was on all of them. As far as I could see his glory was all over the heaven and the earth. He took me from mountain to mountain and all I could see was His presence. I saw mountains of glass which looked like crystals with different shades of color, nothing on earth compared to its beauty. All the mountains represented institutions, government and ruling authorities which made up the kingdom of heaven. They work together to accomplish whatsoever God command. This is one of the reasons why Jesus told his disciples that "This, then, is how you should pray: Our Father in heaven, hallowed be your name, your kingdom come, your will be done on earth as it is in heaven," Matthew 9-10 (NIV). Prayer is an avenue for us to commune with God and for us to see his face. This may not be in the form of visions, but we can hear his voice in the stillness.

God dwells in light and absolutely no one can approach him unless Christ permits it. This scripture came alive to me; Jesus answered, "I am the way and the truth and the life. No one comes to the Father except through me" (John 14:6 NIV). People often pray without acknowledging Christ and some believe that they can go straight to God without Christ. This is a misconception; your prayer must first reach the ear of Christ before it can get to the Father. Our prayers also need to be sincere, coming from a contrite heart. Many people pray but their prayers are not sincere, as such they never reach God. As a result, though many have been praying for years those prayers go unanswered. To get God's attention our prayers must be sincere. "Lord, who shall abide in thy tabernacle? Who shall dwell in thy holy hill? He that walketh uprightly, and worketh righteousness, and speaketh the truth in his heart. He that backbiteth not with his tongue, nor doeth evil to his neighbor, nor taketh up a reproach against his neighbor," Psalm 15:1-3 (KJV).

After showing me the things that the Lord wanted me to see in heaven, he brought me to the throne of Christ and told me that this is where I would stay (at the throne of Christ) and serve as I stand before the gods of the earth.

Ephesians 2:6 (KJV) says, "…(Christ)And hath raised us up together and made us sit together in heavenly places in Christ Jesus."

Prayer changes things, and a believer reigning with Christ should always believe this. By 2019 most of my siblings were born again, except for three of thirteen children. However, we observed that none of us were prospering. The Lord laid it upon my sister's heart to start a prayer group where we would pray for each other, because we were crippled. We were unable to prosper even as born-again believers, our souls were in captivity by the power of darkness. For many years the Lord had been showing me in dreams that I was crippled, I would see myself walking and falling over, I would try to get up but would fall repeatedly. At the time, no matter what I did I just could not get ahead in life. If I worked and saved twenty thousand dollars, in no time I would be out of a job until the money I had saved was depleted. At one point my house was in foreclosure because I could not afford to pay my mortgage and there was no one to help me. I had hit the lowest low, but I remained faithful in prayer. I never complained to a soul, I sought after my Father. When my sister called for a month of fasting, I was happy to be a part of it because my life was going nowhere, and I needed answers. We all joined in unity for that month of prayer and fasting. This was the life our parents demonstrated before us when we were young. Growing up prayer was the lifeline and heartbeat of our home. All of us had learned how to pray from an early age, this is one of the best ways to help your family thrive. When you pray together, each member of the family learns what it means to be intimate with God. When you see answers to prayers, you experience his love and his presence in your daily life. My mother told me the story of how my father had gotten sick while working. She was a stay-at-home mom and without his income they could not pay their rent, so they had to give up the house and move in with her mother for a while. The rest of my mother's family was disgruntled over the idea of him being there, so they had to move again. Mama got down on her knees and asked the Lord to heal her husband, the next day he got up and went to work. That is the power of prayer. We should demonstrate a life of prayer before our children. One evening when my parents did not have anything for dinner, Mother asked the Lord to send help. By faith she put the pot on the fire, while the water boiled someone came and brought food to cook. I was a young boy by then, so I got to experience that firsthand. Actions speak louder than words. When you demonstrate your faith in front of your family you are leaving a legacy for them to follow.

Our family prayers as siblings got so successful over the kingdom of darkness that it changed our lives, so much so that our children now rely on our prayers when they are faced with a problem beyond their control. They now rely on us just as how we relied on our parents when we could not pray for ourselves. Teach your children or child the importance of prayer. Prayers need not be long and technical, teach your family how to talk to God just as they would to you. Prayer has emotional, physical, and mental benefits, studies have proven this. So why would we look any further?

After the month of intense spiritual warfare, we experienced unprecedented breakthroughs. God never loses a battle. When Jacob's descendants were enslaved by the Egyptians, some might have said that God was to be blamed for their misfortune, the fact is he allowed them to go through slavery to make them stronger and that his power might be made known among the Egyptians. We embrace the fact that our parent's relationship with God was not ours, so God allowed the enemy to oppress us so that our hearts could know him. God's wisdom is vastly superior to ours, in that he knows the end from the beginning. He knew what it would take for my family and I to pray, and he allowed circumstances to bring us to him.

Acknowledging Powers of Darkness

Unfortunately, we often think that the only battle we must fight is the devil and never take into consideration the world, the flesh, and the human spirit— we need to be aware of these things and guard our minds lest we become victims to the enemy. "Be alert and of sober mind. Your enemy the devil prowls around like a roaring lion looking for someone to devour," reads 1 Peter 5:8 (NIV). The devil is looking to destroy believers and nonbelievers, by whatever means necessary. Therefore, we must be wise and alert by making daily introspections of our walk with the Lord because the light always exposes the dark whether it comes at noonday or at midnight.

The Lord has shown me that the world is filled with all kinds of spirits and without him humanity would have been lost forever. The world is full of demons and powers of darkness; there is more to the world than what meets the eye. The governing system of this world is pure evil, controlled by the devil and his angels to erase God's program from the hearts and minds of man. Sadly, many are ignorant to this fact. Consequently, they often become tools that the devil uses to destroy those around them. The fact is, Satan cannot destroy God nor man—to try is a waste of time and effort. The devil knows how much God loves man, so he causes man to see man as the enemy while he hides behind them, allowing them to destroy each other.

In our churches today there are many false prophets prophesying lies upon lies and claiming to be called by God. God never calls a false prophet, but Satan does, in order to sabotage God's plan for his people. These prophets go the extra mile to spread their deceit, if you allow these people to speak in your life it will blight your spiritual growth and keep you out of the will of God. Matthew 24:11-14 (KJV) says, "And many false prophets shall rise and shall deceive many. And because iniquity shall abound, the love of many shall wax cold. But he that shall endure unto the end, the same shall be saved. And this gospel of the kingdom shall be preached in all the world for a witness unto all nations; and then shall the end come." If you are a child of God, you will know the voice of God because you are a part of his family." My sheep hear my voice, and I know them, and they follow me: And I give unto them eternal life; and they shall never perish, neither shall any man pluck them out of my hand," John 10:27-28 (KJV). So, although the enemy goes around trying to deceive, if we know God, we will know the deceiver.

Being unknowingly associated with people who are sent by Satan can have devastating effects in your life. It is important to ask the Lord for discernment and revelation as children of God. Not everyone who claims to be a Christian is really a child of God. You must be aware of this, playing of church could be done by your pastor, your best friend, whomever makes themselves available can be the tool the devil uses against you. The Lord showed me that therefore he gave us the Holy Spirit, to guide us in this world. We must welcome his presence in everything we do, so that we can accomplish our purpose on earth.

I began to seek the Lord with deep earnestness about a year ago, I told him that I was sick of where I was spiritually, and I asked him to take me to the secret place. Every sin the Lord brought to my memory I repented of it. There were somethings I struggled to let go of, because my mind was enticed by the things of this world. God had to chip away the cares of this world to reshape my life for His glory. Though the powers of hell and darkness may try to oppress our lives, our focus must be on God. The following weekend my sister came over to see me and told me to press into God because he heard my prayer. This assured me that he heard my cry.

Christ's blood gives us power over the devil, with such power comes responsibilities to show forth the power of the blood and to keep Satan out of our lives. Satan fears the blood of Jesus, it reminds him of his defeat and the believer's right to the throne of God. Revelation 12:11 (KJV) says, "And they overcame him by the blood of the Lamb, and by the words of their testimony, and they loved not their lives unto the death." The blood washes, cleanses, purifies, heals, guides, and protects us from all evil, harm, sicknesses, it blesses and makes us as holy unto the Lord. Through his most precious blood and his most holy wounds, we are saved form sin.

Demons and Witchcraft Exist but We Are Not Defeated

According to scripture, Satan and one-third of the hosts of heaven were cast out of heaven where God dwells. Because he wanted to be God in the place of the Almighty, but God would not allow that. There can be but one God, one ruler of the universe. "How art thou fallen from heaven, O Lucifer, son of the morning! how art thou cut down to the ground, which didst weaken the nations! For thou hast said in thine heart, I will ascend into heaven, I will exalt my throne above the stars of God: I will sit also upon the mount of the congregation, in the sides of the north: I will ascend above the heights of the clouds; I will be like the Highest. Yet thou shalt be brought down to hell, to the sides of the pit (Isaiah 14:12-15 KJV).

Satan was cast out with all the angels that rebelled against God. His activities are all over the world. Many people, like the falling angels, side with Satan to do evil because they are evil.

A young man who lived in the rural area of Africa, in a time when very few people practiced their Christian faith, went blindly into a relationship with a woman who was involved in witchcraft without his knowledge, until it began to affect his life. His family were Christians and loved the Lord as such he was brought up in the fear of the Lord. The Lord told him not to marry this woman nor to get involved with her, her mother and grandmother were involved in witchcraft, but he did, nonetheless. He saw her as a person he could have a relationship with, but the Lord knew her as someone else. The seed of evildoers were planted in her through her bloodline. It is important for everyone to listen to the voice of the Lord. Whenever God almighty speaks to us about getting involved with people, we must obey him. Whether he speaks through prayer or someone else who prays. He knows the end from the beginning and what is best. Sometimes we cause curses in our own lives because of the family we join ourselves to, without God's approval, and then end up losing more than we gain; this young man was a perfect example of this.

He was young, disobedient, and naïve, thinking that this woman was the best thing that happened to him. It is funny how life can throw you a curveball just when you think that you have the best, the worst hits you in the face like a tornado removing everything in its path. Yes, this was what happened to the young man because he thought that he knew more than God. He listened to no good advice. Even the dead spoke to him and asked him what he was doing in that family, that it was not the place for him, but that did not change his decision. The woman got pregnant and that changed his life for a very long time. When this happened, it put a cap on his life. The events caused him to realize that he was out of connection with God, and everything was spiraling out of control. Not only did he let his family down by not being a godly example, but he also let God down. His decision caused him to walk out of God's will for his life and his life became a rolling stone, until God stepped in.

He decided to talk to his pastor about the situation that was taking place in his life. The pastor told him that if he stayed with this woman his life would not progress. Light and darkness cannot walk together. Sometimes we think that God is going to bless ungodly marriages, he cannot. We cannot change the word of God to suit us, we must obey the word of God. Ahab joined himself to Jezebel in marriage and, it brough about destruction in Israel. 1 Kings 17:1 KJV reads, "And Elijah the Tishbite, who was of the inhabitants of Gilead, said unto Ahab, "As the LORD God of Israel liveth, before whom I stand, there shall not be dew nor rain these years, but according to my word."

He shared how he was under intense mind control, it felt like someone was navigating his life. He found himself doing things he would not ordinarily do because he constantly heard voices in his head. He had to make sure that he was always on his her "good side." If he got her upset, he could not sleep at night because a tormenting spirit would oppress him. If she asked him for money even if he did not have it at the time, he had to make sure she got it. He described his experience comparing it to someone stabbing him in the head and that the feeling would not leave until he did as she wanted. He told his family what was happening, but no one believed him. The Holy Spirit revealed to me that this is how the devil works, he does things and make it appear or feel as though you are out of your mind. Many of our churches pretend as though demons do not exist. Let me assure you, they do, and you are not out of your mind like they want you to believe, you are perfectly sane. Because they are lukewarm, many believers are suffering from witchcraft and demonic oppression unbeknownst to them.

The Bible confirms the existence of demons several times in both the Old and New Testaments. 1 Samuel 16:13-15 (KJV)reads, "Then Samuel took the horn of oil and anointed him in the midst of his brethren: and the Spirit of the Lord came upon David from that day forward. So, Samuel rose up, and went to Ramah. But the Spirit of the Lord departed from Saul, and an evil spirit from the Lord troubled him. And Saul's servants said unto him, Behold now, an evil spirit from God troubleth thee."

1 Kings 22:19-23(NIV) reads, "Micaiah continued, 'Therefore hear the word of the Lord: I saw the Lord sitting on his throne with all the multitudes of heaven standing around him on his right hand and on his left.' And the Lord said, 'Who will entice Ahab, into attacking Ramoth Gilead and going to his death there?' One suggested this, and another that. Finally, a spirit came forward, stood before the Lord and said, 'I will entice him.' 'By what means?' the Lord asked.' 'I will go out and be a deceiving spirit in the mouths of all his prophets,' he said. 'You will succeed in enticing him,' said the Lord. 'Go and do it.' So now the Lord has put a deceiving spirit in the mouths of all these prophets of yours. The Lord has decreed disaster for you.'"

Luke 8:30-33(KJV) says, "and Jesus asked him, saying, what is thy name? And he said, Legion: because many devils were entered into him. And they besought him that he would not command them to go out into the deep. And there was there a herd of many swine feeding on the mountain: and they besought him that he would suffer them to enter into them. And he suffered them. Then went the devils out of the man and entered into the swine: and the herd ran violently down a steep place into the lake and were choked."

Again, in the New Testament, Acts 16:16-18 (KJV)says, "And it came to pass, as we went to prayer, a certain damsel possessed with a spirit of divination met us, which brought her masters much gain by soothsaying: The same followed Paul and us, and cried, saying, these men are the servants of the most high God, which shew unto us the way of salvation. And this did she many days. But Paul, being grieved, turned and said to the spirit, I command thee in the name of Jesus Christ to come out of her. And he came out the same hour."

People are not only possessed by demons but there are everyday people who practice witchcraft and who worship Satan.

The Lord eventually blessed him with a wonderful wife, he often boasts about how he could not have asked for a better woman than Kate. He was also blessed with two other children, a total of three amazing children whom he loves dearly. He and Kate celebrated their tenth anniversary in grandeur, amazed at where the Lord had brought them. The Lord had used his wife to bring healing to his life in many ways. He thought that he would never get involved in another relationship because of the hurt he had experienced in the past, but when the Lord told him that she was his wife he felt the peace of God and the need for someone in his life. After all, God said it is not good for a man to be alone, therefore he brought Eve to Adam and they became one flesh. Only heaven knows where he would be without his wife, he believes when God was creating her, he had him in mind. A good woman is hard to find, and I believe God wanted one who loved the Lord the way this young man does or even more, for him. He had prayed and asked the Lord for someone who loves and trusts him, and he answered his prayers. A good wife is like a diamond, someone special, who uniquely fits into your life without leaving room for wanting anyone else. Proverbs 31:10-12(NIV) reads, "A wife of noble character who can find? She is worth far more than rubies. Her husband has full confidence in her and lacks nothing of value. She brings him good, not harm, all the days of her life." He and his wife have been together for a relatively short time, but the love they have for each other is as fresh as yesterday, and every day seems to get better. It is clear to see that their marriage has God, love, and respect for each other. I am not an expert at marriage, but I know that when God put two people together it will last a lifetime if you allow him to be the center of it all.

Even though things had been better for them he felt the need for prayer and fasting to release him from the grip of his past relationship. So, he asked his friends and family to join him in prayer. It is important to surround yourself with likeminded believers, who can pray for and with you, community is very important in the kingdom. The word of God in Deuteronomy 32:30-33 (KJV) says, "How should one chase a thousand, and two put ten thousand to flight, except their Rock had sold them, and the LORD had shut them up? For their rock is not as our Rock, even our enemies themselves being judges. For their vine is of the vine of Sodom, and of the fields of Gomorrah: their grapes are grapes of gall, their clusters are bitter: Their wine is the poison of dragons, and the cruel venom of asps." At times this young man would go home and feel as though someone else was living in their home. He would feel and see spirits walking around, he would plead the blood of Jesus and they would leave for a while, but by nightfall they would be back. He and his wife would pray but they got the same results repeatedly. It got so bad that their children were afraid to sleep in their rooms because they were having nightmares. They concluded that their prayers were going unanswered or as though they lacked the power needed to bring an end to this problem that was making their home uncomfortable.

We are in a spiritual war that we do not hear much about in churches, but it is real. I hope the stories I share will enlighten your understanding of what is going on around you and what others are experiencing. The presence of evil is all over and it seems that some of our spiritual leaders are spiritually blind or they are just siding with the devil. As the young man's friends and family interceded, one of them asked him, who the people were who were walking up and down as if they were gods in his house. All this time he was rebuking demons, believing it was unclean spirits because they were in the form of human spirits, while in fact they were humans coming out of their bodies and entering his home. No one in church teaches us about how witches come out of their bodies and enter people's houses, bringing about harm and destruction in families around the world. No one teaches us how to deal with them in the spirit and as a result many of God's people are crippled by these evil workers while they hide behind demons. This was what these people were doing to this young man and his family. When he left the previous relationship, that was the best thing he ever did. That woman and her mother vowed to destroy his life no matter what it took on their part. These were people who sit on the choir and participate in church but are only there to cover up their evil ways. God sees their evil works and he will pay every man based on his works. But God always delivers his people, despite our failures, he still fights for those who trust him. God has been more than a friend to us, he is our Father, friend, and defense. Whenever a curse is against you, you will find it difficult to prosper because the demonic world works together to bring about failure in people's life. There are no mountains too high for God to bring down, no problems too hard for him to solve and no ocean too wide for him to cross. He is all powerful and he never loses a battle.

The devil and witches work together to bring about harm to people while painting a picture as if they are losing their minds or make it seem as if they do not exist. Believe me, they do exist more than ever. We can define witchcraft as a supernatural means to cause harm, death, or misfortune, while magic also belongs to the field of supernatural, or at least esoteric knowledge, but can be used to less dangerous effects: like divination and astrology. No matter the name people give them, they are satanic to the core and should never be publicly allowed in society. In the United States satanism is openly practiced which is more dangerous than when a person takes a gun and shoots someone. The police can chase the gun and find the killer, but when dealing with witches what are they to chase? There is no evidence, but many people die by the hands of witches or suffer severe loss and pain.

For over twelve years the young man's life was oppressed by Satan. Some might ask, why we are attacked as Christians? But remember, Eve was first attacked by Satan, and because she and Adam sinned—we are all vulnerable to attacks of the enemy, the word says in 1 Peter 5:8 (KJV):"Be sober, be vigilant; because your adversary the devil, is like a roaring lion, walketh about, seeking whom he may devour." Often people open themselves for Satan to work through them, even the closest person to you might be a tool for Satan against you. Therefore, our spiritual eyes must be open to prevent us from the traps of Satan.

God warned him not to get involved with these people, because he knew their evil practices—but he disobeyed. This opened the door for Satanic attacks because he voluntarily disobeyed God's warning. When God does allow Satan or his demons to attack a person, there are reasons for it. Job did not see why God allowed Satan to attack him, Job 1:12 (KJV): "And the Lord said unto Satan, Behold, all that he hath is in thy power; only upon himself put not forth thine hand. So, Satan went forth from the presence of the Lord." I believe God uses situations like these to thwart Satan's boasts and to bring glory to the Lord. God allows us to go through the fire so that our spiritual eyes might be opened to the supernatural. As a Pastor I encounter people who are bound by the powers of darkness and immediately through the spirit I can tell whether it is satanic related or if it is of natural causes.

In our home we pray regularly; my wife and I make prayer a lifestyle. One night while praying I lifted my hands to heaven and the Spirit of the Lord descended through my hands, down my arm and into my body and the Lord said to me, "From now on, whosoever you lay your hands on to pray for, if they are oppressed by demons or witchcraft, you will be able to discern and destroy it." From that night on I have been operating in that anointing. One Sunday morning after I finished preaching, the saints came for prayer and as I laid my hand on a brother, I saw in the spirit that a snake was wrapped around him. He was bound in the spirit but was immediately loose. God will allow demonic attacks for several reasons, including to test us, to build our intimacy with him or to develop our community with other believers. But through all this, he has promised never to leave us. All these workings are for us to endure, so that we can reign with Christ in eternity.

Evil resides in many churches now more than ever, some pastors are in the occult and some members as well. As soon as they see God's hands on you, they'll try to kill your spirit to prevent the presence of the Lord. All over the world you find these evil workers hijacking the church of God, believing that they are doing God's services but, they are servants of the devil, see Ezekiel 34:2-10. I grew up in a church that took authority over darkness, not the other way around. People of God we must take authority over the gates of hell, Christ has given us the power to do so. It makes my heart bleed to see what we have become as the church. We were once filled with power, now we are a church without power. Jesus said in Matthew 16:18 (KJV), "And I say also unto thee, that thou art Peter, and upon this rock I will build my church; and the gates of hell shall not prevail against it."

Satan can only prevail if we let him. One of his most effective strategies against the church and people is open-mindedness. When you are too open-minded, you end up doing things out of the will of God and this gives way to the devil. For example, some Christians listen to rock-and-roll music and watch R-rated movies while others go to the psychic for answers, while some are members of secret societies. Light and darkness cannot walk together. If a member in the church is not following the principles of Christ, he or she is not in the faith and therefore is a hinderance to the church especially when it is coming from the leader. Achan as a leader of his house sinned against God, he said, "When I saw among the spoils a goodly Babylonish garment, and two hundred shekels of silver, and a wedge of gold of fifty shekels weight, then I coveted them, and took them; and behold, they are hid in the earth in the midst of my tent, and the silver under it" Joshua 7:21 (KJV). The Israelites lost the next battle even though God promise to be with them. They broke covenant by allowing sin to come in the camp, because of that they were beaten and killed by a small army. It is the same way many are deceived by Satan in church today. The outcome is the church stands for nothing, we are silent on major issues like abortion and same-sex marriages, everyone is saying leave it to God to fix. God not only saves us to pray in our closets, but to bring change in the world. The enemy and his agents are out to destroy the world and we must be a force to reckon with.

Hell Should Not Be Where We Spend Eternity

In a vision the Lord showed me two spirits of death with responsibility to take people to hell. When people die without Christ they rejoice. They take pleasure in seeing people in pain and suffering; each time someone cried they laughed—it gave them pleasure. John 10:10(KJV) says, "The thief cometh not, but for to steal, and to kill and to destroy I am come that they might have life, and that they might have it more abundantly." I heard the voices of people who had been crying for more than a thousand years but could not die. They were more alive than ever, in pain, begging God to let them out of hell.

Hell is sealed and no one can escape its wrath and indignation against the sins of men, once they are sentenced there. The horror of hell is worse than anything you have ever seen. What makes it powerful is its absoluteness. Those condemned to it can remember the life they lived on earth with much regret and remorse, but it is useless, since nothing can be changed once in hell—it is final.

Luke 16:19-24 (KJV) tells us of the story of the rich man begging for water while in hell, he asked for water from the tip of Lazarus' finger to cool his tongue. What extremity of desperation if he only required a tip of water? The most abundant liquid on earth is unavailable in hell, there is no sleep to rejuvenate the soul nor the pleasures of life. They were all gone, forever.

Some people speak of hell as if it is merely a second home, where they will be reunited with their loved ones and friends. But the surprise is on them since they will meet all those who turned their backs on the mercies of God, the murderers, thieves, homosexuals, drunkards, liars, false prophets, false preachers, law breakers and false accusers. All sin whether we think them big or small will be punished by sentence to the lake of fire, if the sinner does not repent and turn to God for salvation there shall his eternity be.

Hell is a place where the fire continues to burn and worms feed on the human flesh. A place where men long for death, but death is not near. It is a place of constant torment and sorrow, without end. "Then he (the rich man) said, I pray thee therefore, father, that thou wouldest send him to my father's house: For I have five brethren; that he may testify unto them, lest they also come into this place of torment. Abraham saith unto him, they have Moses and the prophets; let them hear them and he said, Nay, Father Abraham: but if one went unto them from the dead, they will repent. And he said unto him, if they hear not Moses and the prophets, neither will they be persuaded, though one rose from the dead," see Luke 16:27-31 (KJV).

All that we do are naked and open before God. Therefore, if you believe that God is just and will punish all sins and refuse to live holy, you will be asked to give an account on the day of judgment. Ecclesiastes 12:14(NIV) says, "For God will bring every deed into judgment, including every hidden thing, whether it is good or evil. Therefore, we should live holy lives, lives free from sin and in line with God."

It is vain to trust in yourself and not in God. People all around the world believe that they are their own gods, they do not want to be subjected to a higher power, hence there is no need for a supreme God. These are just a few of Satan's lies to control their lives. The moment you start believing his lies you become his slave. Eve believed his lies that she would not die, and so she saw it as an opportunity to become like God, without knowing that she was already like her creator. God made us just the way he wanted us to be, in his own image and likeness but the devil always seeks to change the plan of God for our lives. You must look out for these lies, otherwise you may fall for them, and think they are God's plan for you. "For I know the plans I have for you, declares the Lord, plans to prosper you and not to harm you, plans to give you hope and a future. Then you will call on me and come and pray to me, and I will listen to you. You will seek me and find me when you seek me with all your heart," says Jeremiah 29:11-13(KJV).

CHAPTER FIVE
Reigning with Christ in Eternity

We have been challenged to reign with Christ in our daily lives, to die to the flesh and our will, to live boldly in his redeeming blood and the good life he has for us, while enduring the attacks of the enemy. If we do so, and consistently try to do so, then we should reign with Christ in eternity. He said he has gone to prepare a place for us, and our mission should be to prepare for that place. We have to be counted worthy of our calling and of the promise he has left us with.

All things in heaven and on earth except God the Father is subjected to the Lordship of Christ Jesus. His Lordship goes beyond Christianity into the core of all life form, nothing moves without him, Christ is in control. Often times governments and politicians think that they are in control until situations bigger than their advisors and beyond their control arise. It is in those moments when they realize that they are not in control—God is. It is in those moments when they call on the church for support. Furthermore, life would be much easier if we allowed God to play his role in our lives. His role as provider, Father to the fatherless, hope for the hopeless, comforter, counsellor, and friend. Instead, we try to be in control, but make a mess of everything while restricting him from being Lord of our lives. Seeing that all things are put under his feet and all things consist in him in heaven and on earth, who is better qualified to navigate and to govern our lives?

God is all powerful and all things are under His feet. What does this mean for believers? This does not mean that all your problems are over, your worries and insecurities are a thing of the pass. But this sovereignty gives us the right to live and thrive in spite of our problems. We are able to look to God when we feel worried and insecure, making him our hope instead of ourselves. With an outlook that values the source and not the resource, there is little to worry about. Therefore, as a believer you must trust him in spite of what is happening in your life. We believe that God is omnipotent, this means that God is all powerful. He is all powerful over time, space, things, and people. One of the first examples of this as seen in the Bible, was God's creation of the world. Christians also believe that God is omnipresent, he is everywhere at the same time; this ability gives him the advantage to shift things into place. Our lives must measure up to his so that we will always be ready to receive what he is prepared to do.

A man asked me one day, if God is so powerful why is there so much evil in the earth? My answer was this, evil is not a threat to God. While it might be a threat to man it is absolutely not a threat to God. He does not go around wondering what to do with evil. There are only two things that can be done to evil, allow it to run its course or stop it from running its course. God allows it to run its course because he is above it and has the power to destroy it at any time. When you are above your problems you do not waste time trying to fix them. However, there is coming a day when God will stamp it out forever. Revelation 21:4 (KJV) says, "And God shall wipe away all tears from their eyes; and there shall be no more death, neither sorrow, nor crying, neither shall there be any more pain: for the former things are passed away."

We must recognize God as superior and sovereign to all we face on earth and in the heavenlies, until we accept that reality, we will never be able to walk in our authority. Without an acceptance of this reality, we will be burnt-out Christians, fighting battles in the natural, worrying instead of praying, doubting instead of declaring.

Great in the Kingdom of Heaven

If we follow the commandments of God and declare them as God commanded, then we will be called great in the Kingdom, see Matthew 5:19 (KJV). Jesus has promised us a reward in heaven, this should be our daily motivation to live holy lives, to preach the gospel to others and to endure persecution. We cannot imagine what Jesus has gone to prepare for us, but the manifestation of his glory here on earth is but just a foretaste of this. So many of us want to cling to this world and our accomplishments, but can you imagine what heaven is like compared to this life? Let us be new people, fit for heaven, full of righteousness afforded to us by the redemptive blood of Jesus. God seeks to make us his dwelling place, he wants to wipe all tears from our eyes, death shall be no more, neither mourning, God will make all things new and of this we are certain, see Revelations 21:1-5 (KJV). What a glorious day it shall be when we meet our Lord.

Believers, let us hold fast to the hand of God and look up for our redemption draws nigh. I do not have to preach a scary gospel as some like to call it, for us to see how sicknesses and diseases, crime and violence have become rampant in our countries. Lives are being snuffed out at the drop of a pin. People are dying, leaving behind their spouses, careers, houses, cars and all the things they spent their lives toiling for. Is it worth it in the end? In the end, were the countless hours spent building our temporal lives and neglecting our time in fellowship with God, worth it? One thing is certain, that is, eternity awaits us all. Where will you spend it? The ball is in your court, let every day be a purposeful endeavor to reign in Christ.